CHATS ON
OLD FURNITURE

A PRACTICAL GUIDE FOR COLLECTORS

BY

ARTHUR HAYDEN

AUTHOR OF "CHATS ON ENGLISH CHINA,"
"CHATS ON OLD SILVER," ETC.

ERNEST BENN LIMITED
LONDON

First Edition	.	.	.	.	1905
Second ,, (	.	.	.	.	1906
Third Impression		.	.	.	1907
Third Edition (Fourth Impression)					1909
Fifth Impression .		.	.	.	1912
Sixth ,,	.	.	.	.	1913
Seventh ,,	.	.	.	.	1915
Eighth ,,	.	.	.	.	1916
Ninth ,,	.	.	.	.	1917
Fourth Edition (Tenth Impression)					1920
Eleventh Impression		.	.	.	1921
Twelfth ,,		.	.	.	1923
Thirteenth ,,		.	.	.	1925
Fourteenth ,,		.	.	.	1928
Fifteenth ,,		.	.	.	1929
Sixteenth ,,		.	.	.	1947

JACOBEAN OAK CABINET

Decorated with mother-of-pearl, ebony, and ivory. Dated 1653

Margel L. Sandys
from the
Griffiths
1949.

PUBLISHER'S FOREWORD

THE continued demand for *Chats on Old Furniture*, which went out of print during the war, has made an early re-printing most desirable. Unfortunately under present conditions, and because of the author's recent death, a new edition can be presented only by printing from the existing plates, and any idea of revision must, for the time being, be set aside.

The passage of years has inevitably dated some aspects of the book. In particular the prices quoted by Mr. Hayden are no longer a reliable guide to the collector. We are living in a different money era from that of the pre-war years, and prices tend to be higher in ratio to the reduction in the purchasing power of the pound. But changes in fashion, and the tendency for people to live upon a smaller scale, also influence the prices now paid for particular pieces and particular styles. There is little demand, for example, for large furniture, while small antique pieces are selling to the non-collector in com-petition with the ordinary second-hand furniture which is to-day fetching such absurd prices.

Renaissance oak furniture is not popular to-day and the prices quoted are probably in excess of what the pieces would fetch at the present time. Eighteenth-century furniture grows ever more popular, and Regency and

Empire styles, which were thought little of a few years ago, have gained a considerable following. Indeed, were the author still alive he would probably wish to add a chapter on the furniture of the early nineteenth century to bring the book into line with modern tastes.

Mr. Hayden's warning, in Chapter XII, about the skill of the masters of the gentle art of faking is as necessary to-day as it was when it was written. The faking fraternity are, it seems, always with us, and as the knowledge of expert and amateur collector alike increases the faker grows ever more subtle.

The author, in his preface, also sounds another warning. The danger, to which he refers, of losing our furniture heritage to the U.S.A. is now greater than ever. Taxation is not only breaking up more and more of our great houses, with their incomparable collections of antique furniture, but it is also reducing the numbers of those who can afford to collect at a high level. The auctioneers may look forward to the time when present trading difficulties pass and the American market is again opened up, but those who love English craftsmanship and tradition realise that, if steps are not taken to preserve them, more and more of our treasures will be shipped across the Atlantic, often to be ruined by American steam-heating.

June 1947.

PORTION OF CARVED WALNUT VIRGINAL. FLEMISH SIXTEENTH
CENTURY.

(*At Victoria and Albert Museum.*)

PREFACE

THIS volume has been written to enable those who
have a taste for the furniture of a bygone day to
arrive at some conclusion as to the essential points of
the various styles made in England.

An attempt has been made to give some lucid
historical account of the progress and development
in the art of making domestic furniture, with especial
reference to its evolution in this country.

Inasmuch as many of the finest specimens of old
English woodwork and furniture have left the country
of their origin and crossed the Atlantic, it is time
that the public should awaken to the fact that the

heritages of their forefathers are objects of envy to all lovers of art. It is a painful reflection to know that the temptation of money will shortly denude the old farmhouses and manor houses of England of their unappreciated treasures. Before the hand of the despoiler shall have snatched everything within reach, it is the hope of the writer that this little volume may not fall on stony ground, and that the possessors of fine old English furniture may realise their responsibilities.

It has been thought advisable to touch upon French furniture as exemplified in the national collections of such importance as the Jones Bequest at the Victoria and Albert Museum, and the Wallace Collection, to show the influence of foreign art upon our own designers. Similarly, Italian, Spanish, and Dutch furniture, of which many remarkable examples are in private collections in this country has been dealt with in passing, to enable the reader to estimate the relation of English art to contemporary foreign schools of decoration and design.

The authorities of the Victoria and Albert Museum have willingly extended their assistance in regard to photographs, and by the special permission of the

Board of Education the frontispiece and other representative examples in the national collection appear
as illustrations to this volume.

I have to acknowledge generous assistance and
courteous permission from owners of fine specimens
in allowing me facilities for producing illustrations
of them in this volume.

I am especially indebted to the Right Honourable
Sir Spencer Ponsonby-Fane, G.C.B., I.S.O., and to
the Rev. Canon Haig Brown, Master of the
Charterhouse, for the inclusion of illustrations of
furniture of exceptional interest.

The proprietors of the *Connoisseur* have generously
furnished me with lists of prices obtained at auction
from their useful monthly publication, herein included, and have allowed the reproduction of
illustrations which have appeared in the pages of
the *Connoisseur*.

My thanks are due to Messrs. Hampton, of Pall
Mall, for their kind permission to include as illustrations several fine pieces from their collection of
antique furniture. I am under similar obligation
to Messrs. Waring, who have kindly allowed me to
select some of their typical examples.

To my other friends, without whose kind advice

and valuable aid this volume could never have
appeared, I tender a grateful and appreciative
acknowledgment of my indebtedness.

ARTHUR HAYDEN.

PREFACE TO FOURTH EDITION

IN the present edition eleven new illustrations
have been added, a portion of the letterpress has
been revised and rewritten, and prices of representative examples of the various classes of furniture
obtained at public auction have been added.

September, 1920.   A. H.

SPANISH CHEST. SIXTEENTH CENTURY.

(*In National Archæological Museum, Madrid.*)

CONTENTS

CONTENTS

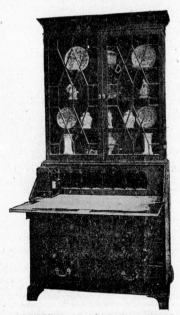

CHIPPENDALE BUREAU BOOKCASE.

Showing secret drawer.

LIST OF ILLUSTRATIONS

BIBLIOGRAPHY

GENERAL.

Ancient Furniture, Specimens of. H. Shaw. Quaritch. 1836. £10 10s., now worth £3 3s.

Ancient and Modern Furniture. B. J. Talbert. Batsford. 1876. 32s.

Antique Furniture, Sketches of. W. S. Ogden. Batsford. 1889. 12s. 6d.

Carved Furniture and Woodwork. M. Marshall. W. H. Allen 1888. £3.

Carved Oak in Woodwork and Furniture from Ancient Houses. W. B. Sanders. 1883. 31s. 6d.

Decorative Furniture, English and French, of the Sixteenth, Seventeenth and Eighteenth Centuries. W. H. Hackett. 7s. 6d.

Ecclesiastical Woodwork, Remains of. T. T. Bury. Lockwood. 1847. 21s.

French and English Furniture. E. Singleton. Hodder. 1904.

Furniture, Ancient and Modern. J. W. Small. Batsford. 1883. 21s.

Furniture and Decoration. J. A. Heaton. 1890–92.

Furniture and Woodwork, Ancient and Modern. J. H. Pollen. Chapman. 1874–5. 21s. and 2s. 6d.

Furniture and Woodwork. J. H. Pollen. Stanford. 1876. 3s. 6d.

Furniture of the Olden Time. F. C. Morse. Macmillan. 12s. 6d.

Gothic Furniture, *Connoisseur*. May, 1903.

History of Furniture Illustrated. F. Litchfield. Truslove. 25s.

Marquetry, Parquetery, Boulle and other Inlay Work. W. Bemrose. 1872 and 1882.

Old Furniture, English and Foreign. A. E. Chancellor. Batsford. £1 5s.

Old Furniture from Twelfth to Eighteenth Century. Wyman. 1883. 10s. 6d.

Style in Furniture and Woodwork. R. Brook. Privately printed. 1889. 21s.

PARTICULAR.

ENGLISH.—Adam R. & J., The Architecture, Decoration and Furniture of R. & J. Adam, selected from works published 1778–1822. London. 1880.

Adam, The Brothers. *Connoisseur.* May, June and August, 1904.

Ancient Wood and Iron Work in Cambridge. W. B. Redfern. Spalding. 1887. 31s. 6d.

Chippendale, T. Cabinet Makers' Directory. Published in 1754, 1755 and 1762. (The best edition is the last as it contains 200 plates as against 161 in the earlier editions. Its value is about £12.)

Chippendale and His Work. *Connoisseur,* January, July, August, September, October, November, December, 1903, January, 1904.

Chippendale, Sheraton and Hepp'ewhite, The Designs of. Arranged by J. M. Bell. 1900. Worth £2 2s.

Chippendale's Contemporaries. *Connoisseur,* March, 1904.

Chippendale and Sheraton. *Connoisseur,* May, 1902.

Coffers and Cupboards, Ancient. Fred Roe. Methuen & Co. 1903. £3 3s.

English Furniture, History of. Percy Macquoid. Published by Lawrence & Bullen in 7s. 6d. parts, the first of which appeared in November, 1904.

English Furniture and Woodwork during the Eighteenth Century. T. A. Strange. 12s. 6d.

Furniture of our Forefathers. E. Singleton. Batsford. £3 15s.

Hatfield House, History of. Q F. Robinson. 1883.

Hardwicke Hall, History of. Q. F. Robinson. 1835.

Hepplewhite, A., Cabinet Maker. Published 1788, 1789, and 1794, and contains about 130 plates. Value £8 to £12. Reprint issued in 1897. Worth £2 10s.

Ince and Mayhew. Household Furniture. N.d. (1770). Worth £20.

Jacobean Furniture. *Connoisseur,* September, 1902.

Knole House, Its State Rooms, &c. (Elizabethan and other Furniture.) S. J. Mackie. 1858.

Manwaring, R., Cabinet and Chairmaker's Real Friend. London. 1765.

Mansions of England in the Olden Time. J. Nash. 1839–49.

Old English Houses and Furniture. M. B. Adam. Batsford. 1889. 25s.

Old English Oak Furniture. J. W. Hurrell. Batsford. £2 2s.

Old English Furniture. Frederick Fenn and B. Wyllie. Newnes. 7s. 6d. net.

Old Oak, The Art of Collecting. *Connoisseur*, September, 1901.

Sheraton, T. Cabinet Maker's Drawing Book. 1791–3 edition contains 111 plates. Value £13. 1794 edition contains 119 plates. Value £10.

Sheraton T. Cabinet Directory. 1803.

Staircases and Handrails of the Age of Elizabeth. J. Weale. 1860.

Upholsterer's Repository. Ackermann. N.d. Worth £5.

FRENCH.—*Dictionnaire de l'Ameublement.* H. Havard. Paris. N.d. Worth £5.

Dictionnaire Raisonné. M. Viollet-le-Duc. 1858–75. 6 vols. Worth £10.

French Furniture. Lady Dilke. Bell. 1901.

French Eighteenth Century Furniture, Handbook to the. Jones Collection Catalogue. 1881.

French Eighteenth Century Furniture, Handbook to the. Wallace Collection Catalogue. 1904.

History of Furniture. A. Jacquemart. Chapman. 1878. 31s. 6d. Issued in Paris in 1876, under the title *Histoire du Mobilier.*

Le Meuble en France au XVI Siècle. E. Bonnaffe. Paris. 1887. Worth 10s.

JAPANESE.—Lacquer Industry of Japan. Report of Her Majesty's Acting-Consul at Hakodate. J. J. Quin. Parliamentary Paper. 8vo. London. 1882.

SCOTTISH.—Scottish Woodwork of Sixteenth and Seventeenth Centuries. J. W. Small. Waterston. 1878. £4 4s.

SPANISH.—Spanish and Portuguese. Catalogue of Special Loan Exhibition of Spanish and Portuguese Ornamental Art. 1881.

GLOSSARY OF TERMS USED

Armoire.—A large cupboard of French design of the dimensions of the modern wardrobe. In the days of Louis XIV. these pieces were made in magnificent style. The Jones Collection at the Victoria and Albert Museum has several fine examples. (See illustration, p. 165.)

Baroque.—Used in connection with over ornate and incongruous decoration as in *rococo* style.

Bombé.—A term applied to pieces of furniture which swell out at the sides.

Boule.—A special form of marquetry of brass and tortoiseshell perfected by André Charles Boule in the reign of Louis XIV. (See Chapter VI., where specimens of this kind of work are illustrated.) The name has been corrupted into a trade term *Buhl*, to denote this style of marquetry. Boule or *Première partie* is a metal inlay, usually brass, applied to a tortoiseshell background. See also *Counter-boule.*

Bureau.—A cabinet with drawers, and having a drop down front for use as a writing-table. Bureaux are of many forms. (See illustration, p. 231.)

Cabriole.—Used in connection with the legs of tables and chairs which are curved in form, having a sudden arch outwards from the seat. (See illustration, p. 143.)

Caryatides.—Carved female figures applied to columns in Greek architecture, as at the Erectheum at Athens. They were employed by woodcarvers, and largely introduced into Renaissance furniture of an architectural character. Elizabethan craftsmen were especially fond of their use as terminals, and in the florid decoration of elaborate furniture.

Cassone.—An Italian marriage coffer. In Chapter I. will be found a full description of these *cassoni.*

Commode.—A chest of drawers of French style. In the chapters dealing with the styles of Louis XIV., Louis XV., and Louis XVI., these are fully described and illustrations are given.

Counter-Boule. Contre partie. — See Chapter VI., where specimens of this work are illustrated. It consists of a brass groundwork with tortoise-shell inlay.

French Polish.—A cheap and nasty method used since 1851 to varnish poor-looking wood to disguise its inferiority. It is quicker than the old method of rubbing in oil and turpentine and beeswax. It is composed of shellac dissolved in methylated spirits with colouring matter added.

Gate-leg table.—This term is self-explanatory. The legs of this class of table open like a gate. They belong to Jacobean days, and are sometimes spoken of as Cromwellian tables.

Gothic. — This term was originally applied to the mediæval styles of architecture. It was used as a term of reproach and contempt at a time when it was the fashion to write Latin and to expect it to become the universal language. In wood-carving the Gothic style followed the architecture. A fine example of the transition between Gothic and the oncoming Renaissance is given (p. 44).

Inlay.—A term used for the practice of decorating surfaces and panels of furniture with wood of various colours, mother-of-pearl, or ivory. The inlay is let into the wood of which the piece inlaid is composed.

Jacobean.—Strictly speaking, only furniture of the days of James I. should be termed Jacobean. But by some collectors the period is held to extend to James II.—that is from 1603 to 1688. Other collectors prefer the term Carolean for a portion of the above period, which is equally misleading. Jacobean is only a rough generalisation of seventeenth-century furniture.

Lacquer. Lac.—A transparent varnish used in its perfection by the Chinese and Japanese. (See "Consular Report on Japanese Lacquered Work," in Bibliography.) Introduced into Holland and France, it was imitated with great success. Under Louis XV. Vernis-Martin became the rage (*q.v.*).

Linen Pattern.—A form of carving panels to represent a folded napkin. This particular design was largely used in France and Germany prior to its adoption here. (See illustration, p. 60.)

Marquetry.—Inlays of coloured woods, arranged with some design, geometric, floral, or otherwise, are classed under this style. (See also *Parquetry.*)

Mortise.—A term in carpentry used to denote the hole made in a piece of wood to receive the end of another piece to be joined to it. The portion which fits into the mortise is called the tenon.

Oil Polish.—Old furniture, before the introduction of varnishes and French polish and other inartistic effects, was polished by rubbing the surface with a stone, if it was a large area as in the case of a table, and then applying linseed oil and polishing with beeswax and turpentine. The fine tone after centuries of this treatment is evident in old pieces which have a metallic lustre that cannot be imitated.

Parquetry.—Inlays of woods of the same colour are termed parquetry work in contradistinction to marquetry, which is in different colour. Geometric designs are mainly used as in parquetry floors.

Reeded.—This term is applied to the style of decoration by which thin narrow strips of wood are placed side by side on the surface of furniture.

Renaissance.—The style which was originated in Italy in the fifteenth century, supplanting the Mediæval styles which embraced Byzantine and Gothic art; the new-birth was in origin a literary movement, but quickly affected art, and grew with surprising rapidity, and affected every country in Europe. It is based on Classic types, and its influence on furniture and woodwork followed its adoption in architecture.

Restored.—This word is the fly in the pot of ointment to all who possess antiquarian tastes. It ought to mean, in furniture, that only the most necessary repairs have been made in order to preserve the object. It more often means that a considerable amount of misapplied ingenuity has gone to the remaking of a badly-preserved specimen. Restorations are only permissible at the hands of most conscientious craftsmen.

Rococo.—A style which was most markedly offensive in the time of Louis XV. Meaningless elaborations of scroll and shell work, with rocky backgrounds and incongruous ornamentations, are its chief features. *Baroque* is another term applied to this overloaded style.

Settee.—An upholstered form of the settle.

Settle.—A wooden seat with back and arms, capable of seating three or four persons side by side.

Splat.—The wooden portion in the back of a chair connecting the top rail with the seat.

Strapwork.—This is applied to the form of decoration employed by the Elizabethan woodcarvers in imitation of Flemish originals.   (See p. 68.)

Stretcher.—The rail which connects the legs of a chair or a table with one another.   In earlier forms it was used as a footrest to keep the feet from the damp or draughty rush floor.

Tenon.—" Mortise and Tenon joint."   (See *Mortise.*)

Turned Work. — The spiral rails and uprights of chairs were turned with the lathe in Jacobean days.   Prior to the introduction of the lathe all work was carved without the use of this tool. Pieces of furniture have been found where the maker has carved the turned work in all its details of form, either from caprice or from ignorance of the existence of the quicker method.

Veneer.—A method of using thin layers of wood and laying them on a piece of furniture, either as marquetry in different colours, or in one wood only.   It was an invention in order to employ finer specimens of wood carefully selected in the parts of a piece of furniture most noticeable.   It has been since used to hide inferior wood.

Vernis-Martin (Martin's Varnish).— The lacquered work of a French carriage-painter named Martin, who claimed to have discovered the secret of the Japanese lac, and who, in 1774, was granted a monopoly for its use. He applied it successfully to all kinds of furniture, and to fan-guards and sticks. In the days of Madame du Pompadour Vernis-Martin had a great vogue, and panels prepared by Martin were elaborately painted upon by Lancret and Boucher. To this day his varnish retains its lustre undimmed, and specimens command high prices.

Woods used in Furniture.

High-class Work. — Brazil wood, Coromandel, Mahogany, Maple, Oak (various kinds), Olive, Rosewood, Satinwood, Sandalwood, Sweet Cedar, Sweet Chestnut, Teak, Walnut.

Commoner Work.—Ash, Beech, Birch, Cedars (various), Deals, Mahogany (various kinds), Pine, Walnut.

Marquetry and Veneers. — Selected specimens for fine figuring are used as veneers, and for marquetry of various colours the following are used as being more easily stained : Holly, Horsechestnut, Sycamore, Pear, Plum Tree.

Woods with Fancy Names.
King Wood, Partridge Wood, Pheasant Wood, Purple Wood, Snakewood, Tulip Wood.

These are more rare and finely-marked foreign woods used sparingly in the most expensive furniture. To arrive at the botanical names of these is not an easy matter. To those interested a list of woods used by cabinet-makers with their botanical names is given in Mr. J. Hungerford Pollen's " Introduction to the South Kensington Collection of Furniture." At the Museum at Kew Gardens and in the Imperial Institute are collections of rare woods worth examination.

I

THE RENAISSANCE
ON THE
CONTINENT

CHATS ON OLD FURNITURE

——•◇•——

I

THE RENAISSANCE ON THE CONTINENT

THE REVIVAL OF LEARNING.

The *ascetic* ideal of human life as probationary, displaced by the *hedonistic* ideal regarding earthly happiness as the highest ideal.

Italy.
1453. Flight of Greek scholars to Italy upon capture of Constantinople by the Turks. Rediscovery of Greek art. Florence becomes the centre of the Renaissance. Leo X., Pope (1475–1521). Leonardo da Vinci (1452–1520). Raphael (1483–1520). Michael Angelo (1474–1564).

France. Francis I. (1515–1547) Henry IV. (1589–1610).
Spain. The crown united under Ferdinand and Isabella (1452–1516). Granada taken from the Moors—1492. Charles V. (1519–1555). Philip II. (1555–1598).
Germany. Maximilian I., Emperor of Germany (1459–1519). Holbein (1498–1543).

The chief periods of English furniture. Foreign influences on English craftsmen. The Renaissance in Italy. The French Renaissance. The Spanish Renaissance. The Flemish Renaissance.

IN attempting to deal with the subject of old furniture in a manner not too technical, certain broad divisions have to be made for convenience

3

in classification. The general reader does not want information concerning the iron bed of Og, King of Bashan, nor of Cicero's table of citrus-wood, which cost £9,000 ; nor are details of the chair of Dagobert and of the jewel-chest of Richard of Cornwall of much worth to the modern collector.

It will be found convenient to eliminate much extraneous matter, such as the early origins of furniture and its development in the Middle Ages, and to commence in this country with the Tudor period. Broadly speaking, English furniture falls under three heads—the Oak Period, embracing the furniture of the sixteenth and early seventeenth centuries ; the Walnut Period, including the late seventeenth and early eighteenth centuries ; the Mahogany Period, beginning with the reign of George III. It may be observed that the names of kings and of queens have been applied to various styles of furniture as belonging to their reign Early Victorian is certainly a more expressive term than early nineteenth century. Cromwellian tables, Queen Anne chairs, or Louis Seize commodes all have an especial meaning as referring to styles more or less prevalent when those personages lived. As there is no record of the makers of most of the old English furniture, and as a piece of furniture cannot be judged as can a picture, the date of manufacture cannot be precisely laid down, hence the vagueness of much of the classification of old furniture. Roughly it may in England be dealt with under the Tudor, the Stuart, and the Georgian ages. These three divisions do not coincide exactly with the periods of oak, of

Portion of carved cornice of pinewood, from the Palazzo Bensi Ceccini, Venice
Italian ; middle of sixteenth century.

Frame of wood, carved with floral scrollwork, with female terminal figures.
Italian ; late sixteenth century.

(Victoria and Albert Museum.)

walnut, and of mahogany, inasmuch as the oak furniture extended well into the Stuart days, and walnut was prevalent in the reigns of George I. and George II. In any case, these broad divisions are further divided into sub-heads embracing styles which arose out of the natural development in taste, or which came and went at the caprice of fashion.

The formation of a definite English character in the furniture of the three periods must be examined in conjunction with the prevailing styles in foreign furniture showing what influences were at work. Many conditions governed the introduction of foreign furniture into England. Renaissance art made a change in architecture, and a corresponding change took place in furniture. Ecclesiastical buildings followed the continental architecture in form and design, and foreign workmen were employed by the Church and by the nobility in decorating and embellishing cathedrals and abbeys and feudal castles. The early Tudor days under Henry VII. saw the dawn of the Renaissance in England. Jean de Mabuse and Torrigiano were invited over the sea by Henry VII., and under the sturdy impulse of Henry VIII. classical learning and love of the fine arts were encouraged. His palaces were furnished with splendour. He wished to emulate the château of Francis at Fontainebleau. He tried to entice the French king's artists with more tempting terms. Holbein, the great master of the German school, came to England, and his influence over Tudor art was very pronounced. The florid manner of the Renaissance was tempered with the broader treatment of the northern school. The art, too, of the Flemish woodcarvers found sympathetic reception in this country, and the harmonious blending of the designs of the Renaissance craftsmen of the Italian with those of the Flemish school resulted in the growth in England of the beautiful and characteristic style known as Tudor.

FRONT OF COFFER. CHESTNUT WOOD. ITALIAN; LATE FIFTEENTH CENTURY.

With shield of arms supported by two male demi-figures terminating in floral scrollwork.

(*Victoria and Albert Museum.*)

The term Renaissance is used in regard to that period in the history of art which marked the return to the classic forms employed by the Greeks and Romans. The change from the Gothic or Mediæval work to the classic feeling had its origin in Italy, and spread, at first gradually but later with amazing rapidity and growing strength, into Germany, Spain, the Netherlands, France, and finally to England.

The Renaissance was in origin a literary movement, and its influence in art came through literature. The enthusiasm of the new learning acting on craftsmen already trained to the highest degree of technical skill produced work of great brilliance.

Never did the fine arts rise to such transcendent heights as in Italy from the fourteenth to the middle of the seventeenth centuries. The late John Addington Symonds, in his work on "The Renaissance in Italy," deals in a comprehensive manner with this memorable period, during which every city in Italy, great or small, was producing wonderful works of art, in painting, in sculpture, in goldsmiths' work, in wood-carving, in furniture, of which now every civilised country struggles to obtain for its art collections the scattered fragments of these great days. "During that period of prodigious activity," he says, "the entire nation seemed to be endowed with an instinct for the beautiful and with the capacity for producing it in every conceivable form."

In the middle of the fourteenth century the Renaissance style in woodwork was at first more evident in the churches and in the palaces of the nobility in the Italian states. Some of the most magnificent examples of carved woodwork are preserved in the choir-stalls, doorways and panelling of the churches and cathedrals of Italy. The great artists of the day gave their talents to the production of woodwork and furniture in various materials. Wood was chiefly employed in making furniture, usually oak, cypress, ebony, walnut, or chestnut, which last wood is very similar in appearance to oak. These were decorated with gilding and paintings, and were inlaid with other woods, or agate, lapis-lazuli, and marbles of various tints, with ivory, tortoiseshell, mother-of-pearl, or with ornaments of hammered silver.

The Victoria and Albert Museum contains some splendid examples of fourteenth and fifteenth century Italian Renaissance furniture, which illustrate well the magnificence and virility of the great art movement which influenced the remainder of Europe. In particular, carved and gilded frames, and marriage coffers (*cassoni*) given to brides as part of their dowry to hold the bridal trousseau, are richly and effectively decorated. The frame of carved wood (illustrated p. 35), with fine scroll work and female terminal figures, is enriched with painting and gilding. The frame on the title-page of this volume is of carved wood, decorated with gold stucco. Both these are sixteenth-century Italian work. In fact, the study of the various types and the different kinds of ornamentation given to these *cassoni* would be an interesting subject for the student, who would find enough material in the collection at the Victoria and Albert Museum to enable him to follow the Renaissance movement from its early days down to the time when crowded design, over-elaboration, and inharmonious details grew apace like so many weeds to choke the ideals of the master spirits of the Renaissance.

The front of the late fifteenth-century coffer (illustrated p. 38) is of chestnut wood, carved with a shield of arms supported by two male demi-figures, terminating in floral scroll work. There are still traces of gilding on the wood.

At first the lines followed architecture in character. Cabinets had pilasters, columns, and arches resembling the old Roman temples. The illustration of a portion of a cornice of carved pinewood appearing as the headpiece to this chapter shows this tendency. The marriage coffers had classic heads upon them, but gradually this chaste style gave place to rich ornamentation with designs of griffins and grotesque masks. The chairs, too, were at first very severe in outline, usually with a high back and fitted with a stretcher between the legs, which was carved, as was also the back of the chair.

In the middle of the fifteenth century Gothic art had attained its high-water mark in Germany before the new art from Italy had crossed the Alps. We reproduce a bridal chest, of the middle of the fifteenth century, from the collection in the Munich National Museum, which shows the basis of Gothic art in England prior to the revival and before further foreign influences were brought to bear on English art (p. 39).

The influence of Italian art upon France soon made itself felt. Italian architects and craftsmen were invited by Francis I. and by the Princesses of the House of Medici, of which Pope Leo X. was the illustrious head, to build palaces and châteaux in the Renaissance style. The Tuileries, Fontainebleau, and the Louvre were the result of this importation. Primaticcio and Cellini founded a school of sculptors and wood-carvers in France, of which Jean Goujon stands pre-eminent. The furniture began gradually to depart from the old Gothic traditions, as is shown in the design of the oak chest of the late fifteenth century preserved in the Dublin Museum, which we illustrate, and commenced to emulate the gorgeousness of Italy. This is a particularly instructive example, showing the transition between the Gothic and the Renaissance styles.

The French Renaissance sideboard in the illustra-

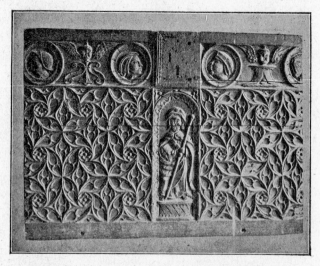

FRONT OF OAK CHEST.   FRENCH ; FIFTEENTH CENTURY.

(*Dublin Museum.*)

tration (p. 45) is a fine example of the middle of the sixteenth century. It is carved in walnut. The moulded top is supported in front by an arcading decorated with two male and two female terminal figures, which are enriched with masks and floral ornament. Behind the arcading is a table supporting a cupboard and resting in front on four turned

WALNUT SIDEBOARD.

FRENCH; MIDDLE OF SIXTEENTH CENTURY.

columns ; it is fitted with three drawers, the fronts of which, as well as that of the cupboard, are decorated with monsters, grotesque masks, and scroll work.

The impulse given by Francis I. was responsible for much decorative work in the early period of the French Renaissance, and many beautiful examples exist in the churches and châteaux of France to which his name has been given. It is noticeable that the chief difference between the Italian and the French Renaissance lies in the foundation of Gothic influence underlying the newer Renaissance ornament in French work of the period. Flamboyant arches and Gothic canopies were frequently retained and mingled with classic decoration. The French clung to their older characteristics with more tenacity, inasmuch as the Renaissance was a sudden importation rather than a natural development of slower growth.

The French Renaissance cabinet of walnut illustrated (p. 48) is from Lyons, and is of the later part of the sixteenth century. It is finely carved with terminal figures, masks, trophies of ornaments, and other ornament. In comparison with the sixteenth-century ebony cabinet of the period of Henry IV., finely inlaid with ivory in most refined style, it is obvious that a great variety of sumptuous furniture was being made by the production of such diverse types as these, and that the craftsmen were possessed of a wealth of invention. The range of English craftsmen's designs during the Renaissance in this country was never so extensive, as can be seen on a detailed examination of English work.

In Spain the Italian feeling became acclimatised more readily than in France. In the sixteenth

CABINET OF WALNUT.

FRENCH (LYONS); SECOND HALF OF SIXTEENTH CENTURY.

Carved with terminal figures, masks, and trophies of arms.

(*Victoria and Albert Museum.*)

century the wood carving of Spain is of exceeding

beauty. The decoration of the choir of the cathedral at Toledo is held to be one of the finest examples of the Spanish Renaissance. In furniture the cabinets and buffets of the Spanish craftsmen are of perfect grace and of characteristic design. The older Spanish cabinets are decorated externally with delicate iron-work and with columns of ivory or bone painted and richly gilded, exhibiting Moorish influence in their character. Many of the more magnificent specimens are richly inlaid with silver, and are the work of the artists of Seville, of Toledo, or of Valladolid. The first illustration of a cabinet and stand is a typically Spanish design, and the second illustration of the carved walnut chest in the National Archælogical Museum at Madrid is of the sixteenth century, when the Spanish wood-carvers had developed the Renaissance spirit and reached a very high level in their art.

Simultaneously with the Italianising of French art a similar wave of novelty was spreading over the Netherlands and Germany. The Flemish Renaissance approaches more nearly to the English in the adaptation of the Italian style, or it would be more accurate to say that the English is more closely allied to the art of the Netherlands, as it drew much of its inspiration from the Flemish wood-carvers. The spiral turned legs and columns, the strap frets cut out and applied to various parts, the squares between turnings often left blank to admit of a little ebony diamond, are all of the same family as the English styles. Ebony inlay was frequently used, but the Flemish work of this period was nearly all in oak.

Marqueterie of rich design was made, the inlay being of various coloured woods and shaded. Mother-of-pearl and ivory were also employed to heighten the effect.

The Italian Renaissance laid a light hand upon the Flemish artists, who, while unavoidably coming under its influence, at first copied its ornateness but subse-

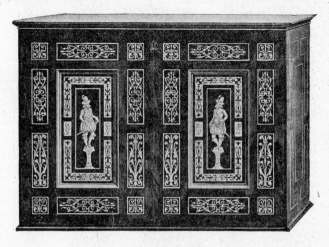

FRENCH CABINET.

Ebony and ivory marquetry work.

MIDDLE OF SIXTEENTH CENTURY.

(*From the collection of M. Emile Peyre.*)

quently proceeded on their own lines. Much quaint figure work, in which they greatly excelled, was used by the Flemish wood-carvers in their joinery. It is grotesque in character, and, like all their work, boldly executed. The influx of foreign influences upon the

Netherlands was in the main as successfully resisted
as is the encroachment of the sea across their land·

SPANISH CABINET AND STAND.   CARVED CHESTNUT；
FIRST HALF OF SIXTEENTH CENTURY.

Width of cabinet, 3 ft. 2 in.; depth, 1 ft. 4 in.; height, 4 ft. 10 in.

(*Victoria and Albert Museum.*)

locked dykes.   The growth of the Spanish power
made Charles V. the most powerful prince in Europe.

Ferdinand of Spain held the whole Spanish peninsula
except Portugal, with Sardinia and the island of
Sicily, and he won the kingdom of Naples. His
daughter Joanna married Philip, the son of Maximilian of Austria, and of Mary the daughter of
Charles the Bold. Their son Charles thus inherited
kingdoms and duchies from each of his parents and

SPANISH CHEST; CARVED WALNUT.

SIXTEENTH CENTURY.

(*In the National Museum, Madrid.*)

grandparents, and besides the dominions of Ferdinand
and Isabella, he held Burgundy and the Netherlands.
In 1519 he was chosen Emperor as Charles V.
Flooded with Italian artists and Austrian and Spanish
rulers, it is interesting to note how the national spirit
in art was kept alive, and was of such strong growth
that it influenced in marked manner the English
furniture of the late sixteenth and early seventeenth
century, as will be shown in a subsequent chapter.

SALE PRICES.

	£	s.	d.
Chest, Gothic, carved with parchemin panels, with a wrought-iron lock, from Nuremburg Castle, German, about 1500. Christie, January 29, 1904	31	10	0
Cabinet, walnut wood, of architectural design, with folding doors above and below and small drawers, carved with arabesque foliage and scrolls in relief, and with columns at the angles, 69 in. high, 38 in. wide, French, middle of the sixteenth century. Christie, April 12, 1904 .	21	0	0
Coffer, oak, the front divided by six buttresses, the steel lock pierced with tracery, 65 in. long, 46 in. high, French, late fifteenth century. Christie, May 6, 1904 . . .	126	0	0
Coffer, large walnut wood, the whole of the front and sides carved in low relief, the lock is rectangular, and pierced with flamboyant tracery, French (provincial), early part of the fifteenth century, 84 in. wide, 36 in. high. Christie, May 6, 1904 .	50	8	0

Coffer, walnut wood, the front and sides
divided into arch-shaped panels
containing Gothic tracery, 86 in.
wide, 32 in. high, French, fifteenth
century. Christie, May 6, 1904   .   52 10 0
Chair, walnut wood, with semicircular
seat, the back composed of six upright rectangular panels, each containing various forms of Gothic
tracery ; below is a longitudinal
panel of tracery, 27 in. wide, 29 in.
high, French or Flemish, fifteenth
century. Christie, May 6, 1904 .   91 7 0
Credence, oak, with folding doors and
drawers above and shelf beneath,
the corners are returned, the various
door panels, &c., carved in low relief ; at the back below is linen fold
panelling, 54 in. wide, 62 in. high,
probably French, early sixteenth
century.   Christie, May 6, 1904   . 336 0 0
Cabinet, walnut wood, in two parts, of
rectangular form, with folding doors
above and below, and two drawers
in the centre, carved with grotesque
terminal figure and gadrooned
mouldings, strapwork and dupli-
cated rosettes, French work, early
seventeenth century, 78 in. high,
48 in. wide. Christie, May 6, 1904 . 110 5 0

£   s.   d.

	£	s.	d.
Cabinet, walnut wood, in two parts, of rectangular form, with folding doors below and above door ; at the sides are terminal male and female figures, the centres of the doors carved, 92 in. high, 49 in. wide, French work (Lyons School), second quarter of sixteenth century. Christie, May 6, 1904 .	99	15	0

II

THE ENGLISH
RENAISSANCE

THE SIXTEENTH CENTURY

By permission of
Messrs. Hampton & Sons.

CARVED OAK CHEST.

ENGLISH; SIXTEENTH CENTURY.

Panels finely carved with Gothic tracery.

II

THE ENGLISH RENAISSANCE

Henry VIII. . . 1509–1547.	
Edward VI. . . 1547–1553.	
Mary . . . . . 1553–1558.	
Elizabeth . . . 1558–1603.	

1525. Hampton Court built.

1566. Increased commercial prosperity. Foundation of Royal Exchange by Sir Thomas Gresham.

1580. Drake comes home from the New World with plunder worth half a million.

1585. Antwerp captured by the Duke of Parma ; flight of merchants to London. Transfer of commercial supremacy from Antwerp to London. Beginning of carrying trade, especially with Flanders.

THE opening years of the sixteenth century saw the beginnings of the Renaissance movement in

England. The oak chest had become a settle with high back and arms. The fine example of an early sixteenth-century oak chest illustrated (p. 59) shows how the Gothic style had impressed itself on articles of domestic furniture. The credence, or tasting

BENCH OF OAK.   FRENCH ; ABOUT 1500.
With panels of linen ornament. Seat arranged as a coffer.
(Formerly in the collection of M. Emile Peyre.)
(*Royal Scottish Museum, Edinburgh.*)

buffet, had developed into the Tudor sideboard, where a cloth was spread and candles placed. With more peaceful times a growth of domestic refinement required comfortable and even luxurious surroundings. The royal palaces at Richmond and Windsor were filled with costly foreign furniture. The mansions

PORTION OF CARVED WALNUT VIRGINAL.

FLEMISH ; SIXTEENTH CENTURY.

(Victoria and Albert Museum.)

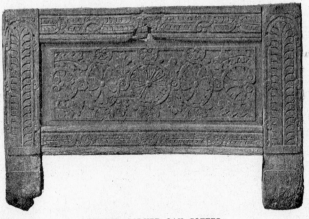

FRENCH CARVED OAK COFFER.

Showing interlaced ribbon work.

SECOND HALF OF SIXTEENTH CENTURY.

(Height, 2 ft. 1 in.; width, 3 ft. 1 in.)

(Victoria and Albert Museum.)

which were taking the place of the old feudal castles
found employment for foreign artists and craftsmen
who taught the English woodcarver. In the early
days of Henry VIII. the classical style supplanted
the Gothic, or was in great measure mingled with it.
Many fine structures exist which belong to this
transition period, during which the mixed style was
predominant. The woodwork of King's College
Chapel at Cambridge is held to be an especially
notable example.

The Great Hall at Hampton Court dates from
1531, or five years after Cardinal Wolsey had given
up his palace to Henry VIII. Its grand proportions,
its high-pitched roof and pendants, display the art of
the woodcarver in great excellence. This hall, like
others of the same period, had an open hearth in the
centre, on which logs of wood were placed, and the
smoke found its way out through a cupola, or louvre,
in the roof.

The roofs of the Early Tudor mansions were
magnificent specimens of woodwork. But the old
style of king-post, queen-post, or hammer-beam roof
was prevalent. The panelling, too, of halls and
rooms retained the formal character in its mouldings,
and various " linen " patterns were used, so called
from their resemblance to a folded napkin, an ornamentation largely used towards the end of the
Perpendicular style, which was characteristic of
English domestic architecture in the fifteenth
century. To this period belongs the superb wood-
carving of the roof and choir stalls of Henry VII.'s
Chapel in Westminster Abbey

The bench of oak illustrated (p. 60) shows a common form of panel with linen ornament, and is French, of about the year 1500. The seat, as will be seen, is arranged as a locked coffer.

FIREPLACE AND OAK PANELLING FROM THE "OLD PALACE"
AT BROMLEY-BY-BOW. BUILT IN 1606.

(*Victoria and Albert Museum.*)

The Elizabethan woodcarver revelled in grotesque figure work, in intricate interlacings of strapwork, borrowed from the Flemish, and ribbon ornamentation, adapted from the French. He delighted in massive embellishment of magnificent proportions. Among Tudor woodwork the carved oak screen of the Middle Temple Hall is a noteworthy example of the sumptuousness and splendour of interior decoration of the English Renaissance. These screens supporting the minstrels' gallery in old halls are usually exceptionally rich in detail. Gray's Inn (dated 1560) and the Charterhouse (dated 1571) are other examples of the best period of sixteenth-century woodwork in England.

Christ Church at Oxford, Grimsthorp in Lincolnshire, Kenninghall in Norfolk, Layer Marney Towers in Essex, and Sutton Place at Guildford, are all representative structures typical of the halls and manor houses being built at the time of the English Renaissance.

In the Victoria and Albert Museum has been re-erected a room having the oak panelling from the " Old Palace " at Bromley-by-Bow, which was built in 1606. The massive fireplace with the royal coat of arms above, with the niches in which stand carved figures of two saints, together with the contemporary iron fire-dogs standing in the hearth, give a picture of what an old Elizabethan hall was like.

Under Queen Elizabeth new impulses stirred the nation, and a sumptuous Court set the fashion in greater luxury of living. Gloriana, with her merchant-princes, her fleet of adventurers on the high seas, and the pomp and circumstance of her troop of foreign lovers, brought foreign fashions and foreign art into commoner usage. The growth of luxurious habits in the people was eyed askance by her statesmen ;

" England spendeth more in wines in one year," com-
plained Cecil, " than it did in ancient times in four

ELIZABETHAN BEDSTEAD.   DATED 1593.

Carved oak, ornamented in marquetry.

(Height, 7 ft. 4 in. ; length, 7 ft. 11 in. ; width, 5 ft. 8 in.)

(*Victoria and Albert Museum.*)

years." The chimney-corner took the place of the
open hearth ; chimneys were for the first time familiar

features in middle-class houses. The insanitary rush-floor was superseded by wood, and carpets came into general use. Even pillows, deemed by the hardy yeomanry as only fit "for women in child-bed," found a place in the massive and elaborately carved Elizabethan bedstead.

The illustration of the fine Elizabethan bedstead (on p. 66) gives a very good idea of what the domestic furniture was like in the days immediately succeeding the Spanish Armada. It is carved in oak; with columns, tester, and headboard showing the classic influence. It is ornamented in marquetry, and bears the date 1593.

All over England were springing up town halls and fine houses of the trading-classes, and manor houses and palaces of the nobility worthy of the people about to establish a formidable position in European politics. Hatfield House, Hardwick Hall, Audley End, Burleigh, Knole, and Longleat, all testify to the Renaissance which swept over England at this time. Stately terraces with Italian gardens, long galleries hung with tapestries, and lined with carved oak chairs and elaborate cabinets were marked features in the days of the new splendour. Men's minds, led by Raleigh, the Prince of Company Promoters, and fired by Drake's buccaneering exploits, turned to the New World, hitherto under the heel of Spain. Dreams of galleons laden with gold and jewels stimulated the ambition of adventurous gallants, and quickened the nation's pulse. The love of travel became a portion of the Englishman's heritage. The Italian spirit had reached England in full force. The poetry and romances of Italy affected all the Elizabethan men of letters. Shakespeare, in his "Merchant of Venice" and his other plays, plainly shows the Italian influence. In costume, in speech, and in furniture, it became the fashion to follow Italy. To Ascham it seemed like "the enchantment of Circe brought out of Italy to mar men's manners in England."

PANEL OF CARVED OAK.

ENGLISH; EARLY SIXTEENTH CENTURY.

Showing interlaced strapwork.

(*Victoria and Albert Museum.*)

The result of this wave of fashion on the domestic furniture of England was to impart to it the elegance of Italian art combined with a national sturdiness of character seemingly inseparable from English art at all periods. As the reign of Queen Elizabeth extended from the year 1558 to the year 1603, it is usual to speak of architecture and furniture of the latter half of the sixteenth century as Elizabethan.

A favourite design in Elizabethan woodwork is the interlaced strapwork (see illustration p. 68), which was derived from similar designs employed by the contemporary stonecarver, and is found on Flemish woodwork of the same period. The panel of a sixteenth-century Flemish virginal, carved in walnut (page 61), shows this form of decoration. Grotesque terminal figures, half-human, half-monster, supported the front of the buffets, or were the supporting terminals of cornices. This feature is an adaptation from the Caryatides, the supporting figures used instead of columns in architecture, which in Renaissance days extended to woodwork. Table-legs and bed-posts swelled into heavy, acorn-shaped supports of massive dimensions. Cabinets were sometimes inlaid, as was also the room panelling, but it cannot be said that at this period the art of marquetry had arrived at a great state of perfection in this country.

It is noticeable that in the rare pieces that are inlaid in the Late Tudor and Early Jacobean period the inlay itself is a sixteenth of an inch thick, whereas in later inlays of more modern days the inlay is thinner and flimsier. In the Flemish examples ivory was often used, and holly and sycamore and box seem to have been the favourite woods selected for inlay.

Days were approaching when furniture was designed for use, and ornament was put aside if it interfered with the structural utility of the piece. Hinges, lock escutcheons, and handles must not be neglected in order to acquire a sound working knowledge of the peculiarities of the different periods

The elaborately carved Court cupboard (p. 74) should be examined. It bears carving on every available surface. It has been " restored," and restored pieces have an unpleasant fashion of suggesting that sundry improvements have been carried out in the process. At any rate, as it stands it is over-laboured, and entirely lacking in reticence. The elaboration of enrichment, while executed in a perfectly harmonious manner, should convey a lesson to the student of furniture. There is an absence of contrast ; had portions of it been left uncarved how much more effective would have been the result! As it is it stands, wonderful as is the technique, somewhat of a warning to the designer to cultivate a studied simplicity rather than to run riot in a profusion of detail.

The illustration (p. 71) shows a fine mantelpiece of the late sixteenth century, bearing the date 1595, when Elizabethan oak carving was in its full splendour. This was removed from an oak panelled room at Great Yarmouth in 1913. The house was on the Old Quay, and was later associated with the regicide William Burton, a bailiff of Yarmouth, and a bitter opponent of Charles I. At the Restoration, when the tide turned, Burton, in common with others, came in for opprobrium, but he was dead. His body was therefore exhumed and burnt by the common hangman, and his name erased from the tablet in the Parish Church at Great Yarmouth, which erasure can be seen to this day. The house where the death warrant of Charles I. was signed is adjacent to this old house.

ELIZABETHAN CARVED OAK MANTELPIECE. DATED 1595.

With fine caryatid figures and richly carved with fruit and foliage.

(Formerly in an Old House at Great Yarmouth.)

DETAIL OF ELIZABETHAN CARVED OAK MANTELPIECE.

(*Illustrated p.* 71.)

Showing bold design of caryatid figure and scrolls in Italianate manner.

The mantelpiece is divided into four compartments, and embellished by terminal caryatide figures carved in a bold manner, and representative of Elizabethan figure ornament, strong and massive in character.

COURT CUPBOARD, CARVED OAK.

ABOUT 1580. (RESTORED.)

(*Victoria and Albert Museum.*)

The decoration is carried out in delicate openwork scrolls in which bunches of grapes and other fruit are introduced.

The massive character of Elizabethan work is

ELIZABETHAN DINING TABLE.

Exhibiting the bulbous form of leg, finely carved.

shown by the dining tables then in use, with bulbous legs and heavy in the understructure, and supports. By the time of James I., the first quarter of the seventeenth century, they lose their bulbous legs and begin to approximate to the oncoming form

By kindness of
T. E. Price, Stretche, Esq

EARLY SEVENTEENTH CENTURY OAK TABLE.
Formerly used as a Communion Table.

by having legs exhibiting another type of turned ornament.

The table which is illustrated above is a typical example of the table in ordinary use in Early Stuart days. This table replaced a stone altar in a church in Shropshire at the time of the Reformation.

It was late in the reign of Queen Elizabeth that upholstered chairs became more general. Sir John Harrington, writing in 1597, gives evidence of this in the assertion that " the fashion of cushioned chayrs is taken up in every merchant's house." Wooden seats had hitherto not been thought too hard, and chairs imported from Spain had leather seats and backs of fine tooled work richly gilded and decorated. In the latter days of Elizabeth loose cushions were used for chairs and for window seats, and were elaborately wrought in velvet, or were of satin embroidered in colours, with pearls as ornamentation, and edged with gold or silver lace.

The upholstered chair belongs more properly to the Jacobean period, and in the next chapter will be shown several specimens of those used by James I.

In Elizabethan panelling to rooms, in chimney-pieces, doorways, screens such as those built across the end of a hall and supporting the minstrels' gallery, the wood used was nearly always English oak, and most of the thinner parts, such as that designed for panels and smaller surfaces, was obtained by splitting the timber, thus exhibiting the beautiful figure of the wood so noticeable in old examples.

SALE PRICES.

	£	s.	d.
Credence, walnut wood, with a cupboard and drawer above and shelf beneath, the corners are returned, the central panel has carved upon it, in low relief, circular medallions, pierced steel hinges and lock, 36 in. wide, 50 in. high, early sixteenth century. Christie, May 6, 1904	346	0	0
Bedstead, oak, Elizabethan, with carved back, dated 1560, and small cupboard fitted with secret sliding panels, and further having carved and inlaid panelled top with inlaid panels, the whole surmounted with heavy cornice. C. W. Provis & Son, Manchester, May 9, 1904	33	0	0
Sideboard, Elizabethan old oak, 6 ft. 2 in. wide by 7 ft. 6 in. high, with carved canopy top ; also fitted with gallery shelf, supported by lions rampant. C. W. Provis & Son, Manchester, May 9, 1904	60	0	0

III

STUART OR JACOBEAN.

EARLY SEVENTEENTH CENTURY

JAMES I., CHARLES I.,
AND COMMONWEALTH

GATE-LEG TABLE.

III

STUART OR JACOBEAN. SEVENTEENTH CENTURY

James I. . . . . 1603–1625.
Charles I. . . . . 1625–1649.
The Commonwealth 1649–1660.

1619. Tapestry factory established at Mortlake, under Sir Francis Crane.
— Banqueting Hall added to Whitehall by Inigo Jones.
1632. Vandyck settled in London on invitation of Charles I.
1651. Navigation Act passed; aimed blow (1572–1652) at Dutch carrying trade. All goods to be imported in English ships or in ships of country producing goods.

WITH the advent of the House of Stuart the England under James I. saw new fashions introduced in furniture. It has already been mentioned that the greater number of old houses which are now termed Tudor or Elizabethan were erected in the days of James I. At the beginning of a new monarchy fashion in art rarely changes suddenly, so that the early pieces of Jacobean furniture differ very little from Elizabethan in character. Consequently the Court cupboard, dated 1603, though bearing the date of the first year of the reign of James, more properly belongs to Tudor days.

In the Bodleian Library at Oxford there is preserved a chair of fine workmanship and of historic memory. It was made from the oak timbers of the *Golden Hind*, the ship in which Sir Francis Drake made his adventurous voyage of discovery round the world. In spite of many secret enemies "deaming him the master thiefe of the unknowne world," Queen Elizabeth came to Deptford and came aboard the *Golden Hind* and " there she did make Captain Drake knight, in the same ship, for reward of his services; his armes were given him, a ship on the world, which ship, by Her Majestie's commandment, is lodged in a dock at Deptford, for a monument to all posterity."

It remained for many years at Deptford dockyard, and became the resort of holiday folk, who made merry in the cabin, which was converted into a miniature banqueting hall ; but when it was too far decayed to be repaired it was broken up, and a sufficient quantity of sound wood was selected from it and made into a chair, which was presented to the University of Oxford. This was in the time of Charles II., and the poet Cowley has written some

OAK CHAIR MADE FROM THE TIMBER OF THE *GOLDEN HIND*.

COMMONLY CALLED "SIR FRANCIS DRAKE'S CHAIR."

(At the Bodleian Library.)

lines on it, in which he says that Drake and his
Golden Hind could not have wished a more blessed
fate, since to " this Pythagorean ship "

" . . . a seat of endless rest is given
To her in Oxford, and to him in heaven —"

*By permission of the
Master of the Charterhouse.*

OAK TABLE, DATED 1616, BEARING ARMS OF THOMAS SUTTON,
FOUNDER OF THE CHARTERHOUSE HOSPITAL.

which, though quite unintentional on the part of the
poet, is curiously satiric.

The piece is highly instructive as showing the
prevailing design for a sumptuous chair in the late
seventeenth century. The middle arch in the back of
the chair is disfigured by a tablet with an inscription,
which has been placed there.

Of the early days of James I. is a finely carved oak
table, dated 1616. This table is heavily moulded and

carved with garlands between cherubs' heads, and shields bearing the arms of Thomas Sutton, the founder of the Charterhouse Hospital. The upper part of the table is supported on thirteen columns, with quasi-Corinthian columns and enriched shafts, standing on a moulded H-shaped base. It will be seen that the designers had not yet thrown off the trammels of architecture which dominated much of the Renaissance woodwork. The garlands are not the garlands of Grinling Gibbons, and although falling within the Jacobean period, it lacks the charm which belong to typical Jacobean pieces.

At Knole, in the possession of Lord Sackville, there are some fine specimens of early Jacobean furniture, illustrations of which are included in this volume. The chair used by King James I. when sitting to the painter Mytens is of peculiar interest. The cushion, worn and threadbare with age, is in all probability the same cushion used by James. The upper part of the chair is trimmed with a band of gold thread. The upholstering is red velvet, and the frame, which is of oak, bears traces of gilding upon it, and is studded with copper nails. The chair in design, with the half circular supports, follows old Venetian patterns. The smaller chair is of the same date, and equally interesting as a fine specimen; the old embroidery, discoloured and worn though it be, is of striking design and must have been brilliant and distinctive three hundred years ago. The date of these pieces is about 1620, the year when the " Pilgrim Fathers " landed in America.

From the wealth of Jacobean furniture at Knole it

CHAIR USED BY JAMES I.

In the possession of Lord Sackville.

is difficult to make a representative selection, but the
stool we reproduce (p. 90) is interesting, inasmuch as

JACOBEAN CHAIR AT KNOLE.

In the possession of Lord Sackville.

it was a piece of furniture in common use. The
chairs evidently were State chairs, but the footstool

was used in all likelihood by those who sat below the salt, and were of less significance.   The stuffed settee which finds a place in the billiard-room at Knole and the sumptuous sofa in the Long Gallery, with its mechanical arrangement for altering the angle at the

By permission of the
proprietors of the "Connoisseur."

JACOBEAN STOOL AT KNOLE.

In the possession of Lord Sackville

head, are objects of furniture difficult to equal.   The silk and gold thread coverings are faded, and the knotted fringe and gold braid have tarnished under the hand of Time, but their structural design is so effective that the modern craftsman has made luxurious furniture after these models.

Carved oak chests were not largely made in

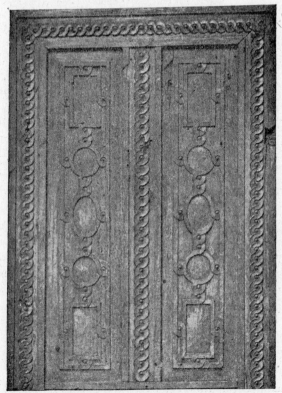

UPPER HALF OF CARVED WALNUT DOOR.

Showing ribbon work.

FRENCH; LATTER PART OF SIXTEENTH CENTURY.

(Height of door, 4 ft. 7 in.; width, 1 ft. 11 in.)

(*Victoria and Albert Museum.*)

Jacobean days—not, at any rate, for the same purpose
as they were in Tudor or earlier times. As church

coffers they doubtless continued to be required, but for articles of domestic furniture other than as linen chests their multifarious uses had vanished. Early Jacobean coffers clearly show the departure from Elizabethan models. They become more distinctly English in feeling, though the interlaced ribbon decoration, so frequently used, is an adaptation from French work, which pattern was now becoming acclimatised. The French carved oak coffer of the second half of the sixteenth century (illustrated p. 61) shows from what source some of the English designs were derived.

In the portion of the French door which we give as an illustration (on p. 91), it will be seen with what grace and artistic excellence of design and with what restraint the French woodcarvers utilised the running ribbon. The ribbon pattern has been variously used by designers of furniture; it appears in Chippendale's chair-backs, where it almost exceeds the limitations of the technique of woodcarving.

Art in the early days of Charles I. was undimmed. The tapestry factory at Mortlake, established by James I., was further encouraged by the " White King." He took a great and a personal interest in all matters relating to art. Under his auspices the cartoons of Raphael were brought to England to foster the manufacture of tapestry. He gave his patronage to foreign artists and to foreign craftsmen, and in every way attempted to bring English art workers into line with their contemporaries on the Continent. Vandyck came over to become " Principal painter of Their Majesties at St. James's," keeping open table at Blackfriars and living in almost regal style. His grace and distinction and the happy circumstance of his particular style being coincident with the most picturesque period in English costume, have won him a place among the world's great painters. Fine portraits, at Windsor and at Madrid, at Dresden and at the Pitti Palace, at the Louvre and in the Hermitage at Petersburg, testify to the European fame of the painter's brilliant gallery representing the finest flower of the English aristocracy, prelates, statesmen, courtiers and beautiful women that were gathered together at the Court of Charles I. and his Queen Henrietta Maria.

The Court of Henrietta Maria at Somerset House, with a fashionable retinue of French retainers, brought expensive tastes, so expensive that Charles sent them all packing, and the King's Guard drove them forth " like so many devils," and they set off to Dover with forty coaches. Their debts in Drury Lane were enormous. But it is undoubted that, in spite of this side of the medal, they must have exercised not a little influence on current taste. In a word, England, under Charles I., was becoming cosmopolitan.

In Early Stuart days the influence of Inigo Jones, the Surveyor of Works to Charles I., made itself felt in woodwork and interior decorations. He was possessed with a great love and reverence for the classicism of Italy, and introduced into his banqueting hall at Whitehall (now the United Service Museum), and St. Paul's, Covent Garden, a chaster style, which was taken up by the designers of furniture, who began to abandon the misguided use of ornament of later Elizabethan

days.   In the Victoria and Albert Museum is an oak
chair with the arms of Thomas Wentworth, first
Earl of Stafford, which, in addition to its historic

ITALIAN CHAIR, ABOUT 1620.
Thence introduced into England.
(*Victoria and Albert Museum.*)

interest, is a fine example of the chair of the period
of Charles I. (illustration facing p. 104).

It is certain that the best specimens of Jacobean
furniture of this period, with their refined lines and

well-balanced proportions, are suggestive of the stately diction of Clarendon or the well-turned lyrics of Herrick.

In the illustration of a sixteenth-century chair in common use in Italy, it will be seen to what source the Jacobean woodworkers looked for inspiration. The fine, high-backed oak Stuart chair, elaborately carved with bold shell and scroll foliage, having carved supports, stuffed upholstered seats, and loose cushion covered in old Spanish silk damask, is a highly interesting example. It was long in the possession of the Stuart MacDonald family, and is believed to have belonged to Charles I.

By permission of
Messrs. Hampton & Son

HIGH-BACK OAK CHAIR.

EARLY JACOBEAN.

Elaborately carved with shell and scroll foliage.

(Formerly in the Stuart MacDonald family, and originally in the possession of King Charles I.)

The gate-leg table, sometimes spoken of as Cromwellian, belongs to this Middle Jacobean style. It cannot be said with any degree of accuracy that in the Commonwealth days a special style of furniture was developed. From all evidence it would seem that the manufacture of domestic furniture went on in much the same manner under Cromwell as under Charles. Iconoclasts as were the Puritans, it is doubtful whether they extended their work of destruction to articles in general use. The bigot had "no starch in his linen, no gay furniture in his house." Obviously the Civil War very largely interfered with the encouragement and growth of the fine arts, but when furniture had to be made there is no doubt the Roundhead cabinetmaker and the Anabaptist carpenter produced as good joinery and turning as they did before Charles made his historic descent upon the House in his attempt to arrest the five members.

There is a style of chair, probably imported from Holland, with leather back and leather seat which is termed "Cromwellian," probably on account of its severe lines, but there is no direct evidence that this style was peculiarly of Commonwealth usage. The illustration (p. 117) gives the type of chair, but the front stretcher is here carved with scrolls.

That Cromwell himself had no dislike for the fine arts is proved by his care of the Raphael cartoons, and we are enabled to reproduce an illustration of a fine old ebony cabinet with moulded front, fitted with numerous drawers, which was formerly the property of Oliver Cromwell. It was at Olivers Stanway, once the residence of the Eldred family. The stand is carved with shells and scrolls, and the scroll-shaped legs are enriched with carved female figures, the entire stand being gilded. This piece is most probably of Italian workmanship, and was of course made long before the Protector's day, showing marked characteristics of Renaissance style (see p. 99).

The carved oak cradle (p. 105), with the letters "G. B. M. B." on one side, and "October, 14 dai," on

EARLY JACOBEAN ARMCHAIR.
With slight indication of crested head.
Dated 1623.

JACOBEAN ARMCHAIR.
With crested and winged head.   Back carved
and decorated with crude marquetry

JACOBEAN ARMCHAIR.
square back ; finely carved panel.   Front
stretcher no longer used.

JACOBEAN ARMCHAIR.
Crested head.   Typical scroll decoration of
the mid-seventeenth century.

the other, and bearing the date 1641, shows the type of piece in common use. It is interesting to the collector to make a note of the turned knob of wood so often

By permission of
Messrs. Hampton & Sons.

EBONY CABINET.

On stand gilded and richly carved.

FORMERLY THE PROPERTY OF OLIVER CROMWELL.

(From Olivers Stanway, at one time the seat of the
Eldred family.)

found on doors and as drawer handles on un-touched old specimens of this period, but very frequently removed by dealers and replaced by metal

handles of varying styles, all of which may be procured by the dozen in Tottenham Court Road, coarse
replicas of old designs.   Another point worthy of
attention is the wooden peg in the joinery, securing
the tenon into the mortice, which is visible in old
pieces.   It will be noticed in several places in this
cradle.   In modern imitations, unless very thought-
fully reproduced, these oaken pegs are not visible.

In the page of Jacobean chairs showing the various
styles, the more severe piece, dated 1623, is Early
Jacobean, and the fine unrestored armchair of slightly
later date shows in the stretcher the wear given by
the feet of the sitters.   It is an interesting piece ; the
stiles in the back are inlaid with pearwood and ebony.
The other armchair with its cane panels in back is of
later Stuart days.   It shows the transitional stage
between the scrolled-arm type of chair, wholly of
wood, and the more elaborate type (illustrated p. 123)
of the James II. period.

In addition to the finer pieces of seventeenth-
century furniture to be found in the seats of the
nobility, such as at Penshurst, or in the manor houses
and homes of the squires and smaller landowners,
there was much furniture of a particularly good
design in use at farmsteads from one end of the
country to the other, in days when a prosperous
class of yeoman followed the tastes of their richer
neighbours.   This farmhouse furniture is nowadays
much sought after.   It was of local manufacture, and
is distinctly English in its character.   Oak dressers
either plain or carved, were made not only in Wales
—"Welsh Dressers" having become almost a trade

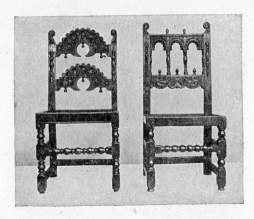

JACOBEAN CARVED OAK CHAIRS.
Yorkshire. about 1640. Derbyshire; seventeenth century.
(*Victoria and Albert Museum.*)

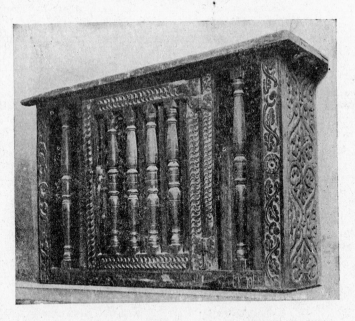

OAK LIVERY CUPBOARD. FIRST HALF OF SEVENTEENTH CENTURY.
In accordance with a Charity founded by Robert Skelton in 1628 to be filled with bread
for public distribution every Sunday.
(*In South Transept of St. Alban's Abbey.*)

term—but in various parts of England, in Yorkshire, in Derbyshire, in Sussex, and in Suffolk. They are usually fitted with two or three open shelves, and sometimes with cupboards on each side. The better preserved specimens have still their old drop-handles and hinges of brass. It is not easy to procure fine examples nowadays, as it became fashionable two or three years ago to collect these, and in addition to oak dressers from the farmhouses of Normandy, equally old and quaint, which were imported to supply a popular demand, a great number of modern imitations were made up from old wood—church pews largely forming the framework of the dressers, which were not difficult to imitate successfully.

The particular form of chair known as the " Yorkshire chair" is of the same period. Certain localities seem to have produced peculiar types of chairs which local makers made in great numbers. It will be noticed that even in these conditions, with a continuous manufacture going on, the patterns were not exact duplicates of each other, as are the machine-made chairs turned out of a modern factory, where the maker has no opportunity to introduce any personal touches, but has to obey the iron law of his machine.

As a passing hint to collectors of old oak furniture, it may be observed that it very rarely happens that two chairs can be found together of the same design. There may be a great similarity of ornament and a particularly striking resemblance, but the chair with its twin companion beside it suggests that one, if not both, are spurious. The same peculiarity is exhibited in old brass candlesticks, and especially the old Dutch brass with circular platform in middle of candlestick. One may handle fifty without finding two that are turned with precisely the same form of ornament.

The usual feature of the chair which is termed " Yorkshire " is that it has an open back in the form of an arcade, or a back formed with two crescent-shaped cross-rails, the decorations of the back usually bearing acorn-shaped knobs either at the top of the rail or as pendants. This type is not confined to Yorkshire, as they have frequently been found in Derbyshire, in Oxfordshire, and in Worcestershire, and a similar variety may be found in old farm-houses in East Anglia.

In the illustration of the three chairs (facing p. 104), the one with arms is of the Charles I. period, the others are later and belong to the latter half of the seventeenth century, where the fashion appears of cane in seats and backs.

The Livery cupboard illustrated (p. 101) is typical, with its turned rails, of mid-seventeenth-century cabinet work. The carving exemplifies the Jacobean floriate style, departing from the set geometric patterns of common usage. Livery cupboards were designed to store victuals, and were the precursors of the modern pantry safe. The example illustrated was filled with bread and distributed to the poor every Sunday under the charity founded by Robert Skelton in 1628.

It is not too much to hope that enough has been said concerning Jacobean furniture of the early and middle seventeenth century to show that it possesses a peculiar charm and simplicity in the lines of its construction, which makes it a very pleasing study to the earnest collector who wishes to procure a few

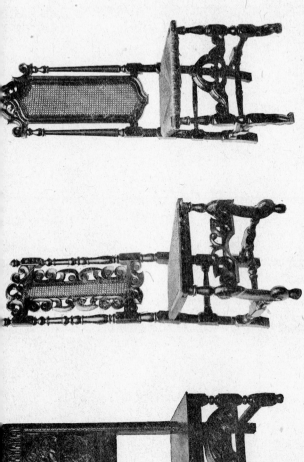

OAK CHAIR.

CHARLES I. PERIOD.

With arms of Thomas Wentworth,
first Earl of Stafford (1593–1641).

WALNUT CHAIR (1660–1685).

CHARLES II. PERIOD.

Panelled cane back and seat.
Finely turned back and stretchers.

(*At Victoria and Albert Museum.*)

WALNUT CHAIR (1685–1689).

JAMES II. PERIOD.

Panelled cane back and rush seat,
Finely turned rails and stretchers.

genuine specimens of old furniture, which, while being excellent in artistic feeling, are not unprocurable by reason of their rarity and excessive cost. It should be within the power of the careful collector, after following the hints in this volume, and after examin-

CRADLE, TIME OF CHARLES I.

CARVED OAK ; WITH LETTERS G. B. M. B.   DATED 1641.

(*Victoria and Albert Museum.*)

ing well-selected examples in such a collection as that at the Victoria and Albert Museum, to obtain, without unreasonable expenditure, after patient search, one or two Jacobean pieces of undoubted authenticity.

SALE PRICES.

£   s.   d.

Cabinet, Jacobean oak, with two drawers, and folding doors below en-
closing drawers, decorated with
rectangular panels in relief, inlaid
in ebony and ivory, and with baluster columns at the side, 48 in. high,
46 in. wide. Christie, November 27,
1903   44   2   0
Chairs, set of three Jacobean oak, with
canework seats, and panels in the
backs, the borders carved with
scrolls, and on scroll legs with
stretchers. Christie, January 29,
1904   52   10   0
Cabinet, Jacobean oak, with drawer
and folding doors below, with
moulded rectangular panels and
balusters in relief, 50 in. high, 46
in. wide. Christie, July 1, 1904 .   35   14   0
Jacobean Oak Bedstead, the head
carved with initials R. L. in panels
with others of marquetry inlay,
and with borders of fluting and interlaced ornament, caryatids, masks
and scrolls, the sunk panels at the
top with inlaid borders, and with
moulded and carved cornice, the

	£	s.	d.
bulbous posts at the foot carved with foliage, and with gadrooned ornament and flutings, 67 in. wide. Puttick & Simpson, February 27, 1920	147	0	0
Jacobean Oak Chest of two drawers, the shaped and sunk panels with moulded borders, on baluster legs and stretcher, 48 in. wide. Puttick & Simpson, February 27, 1920 .	17	17	0
Stuart Oak Chest of Drawers, with large centre drawer, the sunk panels with inlaid and moulded borders, mounted with ivory studs at the corners, and divided by turned mouldings, on ball feet, 40½ in. wide. Puttick & Simpson, May 28, 1920	52	10	0
Charles I. Large Coffer, with raised diamond panels surrounded by small sunk panels, and with an arcaded sunk panel in the centre, mounted with turned studs and divided by mouldings, a long drawer under, on turned feet, 51 in. wide. Puttick & Simpson, May 28, 1920 . .	33	12	0

Oak Buffet, with five drawers and two cupboards, the fronts with raised and sunk panels of different shapes with moulded borders, divided by

turned moulding, and with flutings   £   s   d.
at the corners, on turned legs and
plain stretchers, probably Flemish.
Seventeenth century, 79 in. wide.
Puttick & Simpson, May 28, 1920 .   75   12   0
Charles I. Oak Large Coffer, the front
with raised rectangular panels and
with an arcaded sunk panel in the
centre, divided by turned mouldings, a long drawer under, on bulbous turned feet, 58 in. wide. Put-
tick & Simpson, May 28, 1920   .   52   10   0
Jacobean Oak Refectory Table, the
fluted frieze carved with mouldings,
on six bulbous legs, gadrooned and
fluted, and with square stretchers,
98½ in. long.   Puttick & Simpson,
July 9, 1920   42   0   0
Set of six old Yorkshire Oak Chairs,
with rail backs and solid seats, on
turned legs, with shaped stretchers.
Puttick & Simpson, July 9, 1920   .   26   5   0

IV

STUART OR
JACOBEAN.
LATE SEVENTEENTH CENTURY

CHARLES II., JAMES II., AND
WILLIAM AND MARY

(after picture by Caspar Netscher.)

INTERIOR OF DUTCH HOUSE.
LATTER HALF OF SEVENTEENTH CENTURY.

IV

STUART OR JACOBEAN. LATE SEVENTEENTH CENTURY

Charles II. . . . 1660–1685.
James II. . . . . 1685–1688.
William and Mary . 1689–1694.
William . . . . 1694–1702.

Sir Christopher Wren (1632–1723).
Grinling Gibbons (1648–1726).
1660. Bombay became a British possession. Importation of Indo-Portuguese furniture.

1666. Great Fire in London. Much valuable furniture destroyed.

1675–1710. St. Paul's Cathedral built under Wren's direction.

1685. Edict of Nantes revoked. Spitalfields' silk industry founded by French refugees.

AFTER the Civil War, when Charles II. came into his own again, the furniture of the Restoration period

most certainly took its colour from the gay Court with
which the Merry Monarch surrounded himself.   The

*By permission of the
proprietors of the " Connoisseur."*

CABINET OF THE TIME OF CHARLES II.

With exterior finely decorated with needlework.

cabinet which we reproduce has the royal arms
embroidered on the cover, and is a beautiful example

of intricate cabinetmaking. The surface of the piece
is entirely covered with needlework. On the front

CABINET OF THE TIME OF CHARLES II.

Showing interior and nest of drawers.

stand a cavalier and lady, hand-in-hand. On the
side panel a cavalier is leading a lady on horseback.

On the back a man drives a laden camel, and on another panel is shown the traveller being received by an old man in the grounds of the same castle which appears all through the scenes. This suggests the love-story of some cavalier and his lady. The casket is worthy to have held the love-letters of the Chevalier Grammont to La Belle Hamilton.

As is usual in pieces of this nature, the cabinet contains many artfully devised hiding places. A tiny spring behind the lock reveals one secret drawer, and another is hidden beneath the inkwell. There are in all five of such secret compartments—or rather five of them have been at present discovered—there may be more. The illustration of the cabinet open shows what a nest of drawers it holds.

In the days of plots, when Titus Oates set half the nation by the ears, when James solemnly warned the merry Charles of plots against his life, provoking the cynical retort, "They will never kill me, James, to make you king," secret drawers were no doubt a necessity to a fashionable cabinet.

Catherine of Braganza, his queen, brought with her from Portugal many sumptuous fashions in furniture, notably cabinets and chairs of Spanish and Portuguese workmanship. The cavaliers scattered by the Civil War returned, and as in their enforced exile on the Continent they had cultivated foreign tastes, it was only natural that Dutch, French, and Italian work found its way to this country and effected the character of the early furniture of the Charles II. period. From Portugal came the high-backed chair, having the back and the seat of leather cut with fine design, and coloured or gilded. This leather work is of exquisite character, and we reproduce a portion of a Portuguese chair-back of this period to show the artistic excellence of the design. With Catherine of Braganza came the marriage dower of Bombay, and from India, where the set-tlement of Goa had been Portuguese for centuries, were sent to Europe the carved chairs in ebony, inlaid in ivory, made by the native workmen from Portuguese and Italian models, but en-riched with pierced carv-ing and intricate inlay of ivory in a manner which only an Oriental craftsman can produce. Having become fashion-able in Portugal, they made their appearance in England, and rapidly became popular. At Penshurst Place there are several fine speci-mens of this Indo-Portu-guese work, with the spindles of the chair-

PORTUGUESE HIGH-BACK CHAIR.

Seat and back formed of two panels of old stamped leather, studded with brass bosses.

backs of carved ivory ; and in the Ashmolean Museum at Oxford there is the well-known chair which was presented by Charles II. to Elias Ashmole.

Both in this later Stuart period and in the days of the first Charles inlay was considerably used to heighten the carved designs on oak tables, chairs, and cabinets. The growth of commerce was responsible for the introduction of many varieties of foreign woods, which were used to produce finer effects in marquetry than the rude inlay of Elizabethan days.

The Frontispiece to this volume represents a very handsome cabinet of English workmanship, inlaid with ivory and mother-of-pearl. It is an unusually fine example of the middle seventeenth century, and bears the date 1653, the year when Cromwell forcibly dissolved the Rump Parliament and was declared " Lord Protector of the Commonwealth."

Up till now oak—the hard, tough, English variety, and not the more modern Baltic oak or American varieties now used—was the material for the tool of the carver to work upon. With the introduction of more flowing lines and curves, a wealth of detail, it is not unnatural to find that softer woods began to find favour as more suitable to the new decorations. The age of walnut was approaching when, under William the Dutchman, and in the days of Queen Anne, a newer style of furniture was to arise, made by craftsmen trained in the precepts of Grinling Gibbons and following the conceptions of Sir Christopher Wren. It must be borne in mind that in Italy the softer woods, such as lime, willow, sycamore, chestnut, walnut, and cypress, had long been used for the delicate carving during the height of the Renaissance and succeeding period and in France and Spain chestnut and walnut were favourite woods.

In the central panel of the Restoration chair-back, canework began to be used instead of the Early Jacobean carving. Cane seats were frequent, and loose cushions, attached by means of strings, covered

CROMWELLIAN CHAIR.

Carved oak legs and stretcher. Leather seat and back.

these cane panels and seats.   The illustration (p. 122) shows a Jacobean chair of this period.

Belonging to these later Jacobean days are chests of drawers of oak with finely panelled fronts. We illustrate two specimens, showing the old brass metal work and the drop-handles. They are usually in two parts, and are very deep from back to front. These are two typical examples of this kind of furniture, which was in general use up to the days of Queen Anne, when pieces are frequently found supported on a stand.

In the picture by Caspar Netscher, showing a Dutch lady at her toilet, a good idea is conveyed of the kind of chair in use in Holland in the latter half of the seventeenth century, upholstered in brocade, and the rich tapestry tablecloth is a noticeable feature.

Before entering upon the last phase of Stuart furniture, and leaving the days of Jacobean oak with its fine carving and handsome appearance—the careful result of selecting the timber and splitting it to show the fine figure of the wood—the attention of the reader should be drawn to the fact that the appearance of the surface of furniture made subsequent to this period begins to approach the results of the modern cabinetmaker with his polishes and spirit varnishes and highly glazed panels and table tops. The lover of old oak abominates varnish. The Elizabethan and Jacobean carved oak furniture received only a preliminary coat of dark varnish in its early days, mixed with oil and not spirit, which sank into the wood and was not a surface polish, and was probably used to preserve the wood. These old pieces, which have received centuries of rubbing with beeswax and oil, have resulted in producing a rich, warm tone which it is impossible to copy by any of the subtle arts known to the modern forger. The collector should make himself thoroughly familiar with the appearance of this old oak by a careful examination of museum pieces, which, when once seen, cannot easily be forgotten.

CHEST OF DRAWERS, OAK, LATE JACOBEAN.

(Height, 4 ft. 4½ in.; width, 3 ft. 2 in.; depth, 1 ft. 10 in.)

The Italian Renaissance furniture probably received an oil varnish, the composition of which, like the varnish employed for old violins, has been lost, but after centuries of careful usage and polishing, the result, as seen in the fine specimens in the Victoria and Albert Museum, is to give to them the appearance of bronze.

There is little doubt that the Great Fire, which did such immense destruction in London in 1666, in which some eighty-nine churches and thirteen thousand houses were demolished, gave a considerable impetus to the manufacture of furniture in the new style. It is not a pleasing reflection to think how many fine pieces of Elizabethan and early Jacobean furniture were consumed in the flames, including much of Inigo Jones's work.

Under the genius of Sir Christopher Wren many of the city churches were rebuilt, including St. Paul's Cathedral ; and Greenwich Hospital and Hampton Court were enlarged according to Wren's designs, with the co-operation of the master woodcarver, Grinling Gibbons. In later Jacobean days a splendour of style and an excellence of workmanship were the outcome of the fine achievements in interior woodwork by Grinling Gibbons and the school he founded.

By permission of
Messrs. Hampton & Sons.

CHARLES II. OAK CHAIR.

Open back carved with shell and scrolled foliage. Stuffed seat covered with old damask.

The work of Grinling Gibbons consisted of most natural chains of flowers and foliage, fruit, or birds or cherubs' heads, all faithfully reproduced untrammelled by convention. St. Paul's Cathedral, Hampton Court, Chatsworth, and Petworth House all contain work by him of singular beauty. He trained many assistants to help him to carry on his work, and one of them, Selden, lost his life in endeavouring to save the carved room at Petworth from a destructive fire. The soft wood of the lime was his favourite for detailed carving ; for church panelling or choir stalls, such as at St. Pauls, he employed oak ; in his medallion portraits or figure work he preferred pear or close-grained boxwood.

*By permission of
Messrs. Hampton & Sons.*

CHARLES II. OPEN HIGH-BACK OAK CHAIR.

Finely carved legs and stretcher. Stuffed seat covered in old Spanish silk damask.

The gradual development of the chair in the later Stuart days in the direction of upholstered seat will be noticed in the specimens which are given as illustrations. The revocation of the Edict of Nantes in 1685 by Louis XIV. drove some thousands of French workmen—weavers, glass-workers, and cabinetmakers—to this country. The silk-weaving industry established by them at Spitalfields

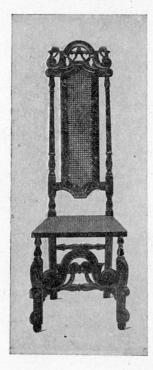

was one of the results, and silk stuffs and brocades were used for covering the seats and backs of furniture. At Hampton Court the crystal glass chandeliers were made by French workmen, whom Wren was glad to employ to assist him to make that palace a worthy rival to Versailles.

The chair here illustrated shows the commencement of the use of cane work in place of wood for the panel in back and for the seat. The James II. chair illustrated shows the later development of the cane-back. The William and Mary chair (illustrated p. 125) shows how the cane-back was retained later than the cane-seat, and how rich damask was employed for the upholstered seat. It is

CHARLES II. CHAIR.

Cane back and seat, finely carved legs and stretcher.

interesting to see how the stretcher, which in earlier days was of use to keep the feet raised from a wet or draughty floor, has now become capable of elaborate

JAMES II. CHAIR.
Carved in walnut, with cane back and seat, and finely turned
legs and stretcher.

ornamentation. Genuine examples of chairs of Elizabethan and Early Stuart days show the wear of the feet of the sitters. The same wear is observable in the lower rail of old tables. In later Stuart days the stretcher has left its place at the bottom, between the two front legs. Since its use as a foot-rest, owing to carpeted floors, is gone, it is found either joining the legs diagonally, or higher up as an ornament with carved front. In the eighteenth century it has almost disappeared altogether.

Mirrors began to take a prominent place in interior decoration. The house of Nell Gwynne in St. James's Square had one room entirely lined with glass mirrors. Hampton Court is full of mirrors, and they are arranged with considerable skill. By an artful arrangement the mirror in

WILLIAM AND MARY CHAIR.

Cane back. Seat upholstered in damask. Finely carved legs and stretcher.

the King's Writing Closet is placed at such an angle that the reflection of the whole suite of rooms may be seen in it. The looking glasses made in this

9

country in the late seventeenth and early eighteenth centuries were the work of Venetian and French workmen. The plates had a bevel of an inch in width, and these bevels followed the shape of the frame, whether square or oval. A factory was established near Battersea which produced some fine work of this nature. It will be noticed by the collector who is observant that the bevels differ considerably from modern bevels. The angle is not such an acute one, and sometimes the edges are double bevelled. Many of the mirrors of the time of William and Mary had an ornamented border of blue glass. Sometimes the mirror was painted with festoons of flowers and with birds in French manner. In imitation of Italian style the back of the mirror, in examples a little later, was worked upon in the style of intaglio, or gem cutting, this presenting a dull silver surface when seen from the front.

In picture frames, in chimneypieces, or in mirror frames the school of Grinling Gibbons was still preeminent in carving. Now and again are found traces of Italian or Louis XIV. influence, but as a whole the English carver held his own, and the traditions of Grinling Gibbons were maintained, and he did not easily allow himself to be carried away by foreign elaborations.

When William of Orange came over in 1688 he brought with him many of his own countrymen as military and civil advisers, and in their train came artists and craftsmen, who introduced Dutch art into England, and prepared the way for the more homely

style of Queen Anne. Walnut cabinets inlaid with
various woods, and with ivory squares representing miniature Dutch courtyards in the recesses of
cabinets, had found their way into England. With
the period of William and Mary the cabriole leg in
chairs and in tables became popular—at first an
English adaptation of Dutch models—but later to
develope into the glorious creations of the age of
walnut.

Blue delft jars and bowls, some especially made for
William and Mary and bearing the Royal arms and
the cypher " W. M. R." and the Nassau motto,
"*Je main tien-dray*,' still to be seen in the Queen's
Gallery at Hampton Court, were introduced, and it
became fashionable to collect china. Consequently
the furniture in rooms had to be adapted for the
arrangement of this new class of ornament, and
cabinets were largely made with accommodation to
receive vases and beakers and blue bowls on their
shelves. The earlier form have straight sides ; but
later, especially in the next reign, they follow French
designs, and are swollen or *bombé* at the sides.

With William, too, came over the plain walnut
card-table. Clock cases of the style termed " Grandfather" were of Dutch origin. The seats of chairs
were shaped and removable. The Dutch trade with
the East Indies had brought Oriental china and lac
cabinets into Holland, and these, with the coming of
William, found their way into this country. Bureaux
with a number of secret recesses were introduced,
and another Dutch importation from the East was
the now celebrated chair or table leg with claw and

ball foot. This came directly from China, and as in the case of delft, which is the earthenware replica by the Dutch potter of fine blue porcelain vases, from Nankin and Canton, where the Oriental perspective and design have been slavishly copied, so

UPPER PORTION OF CHAIR BACK OF CUT LEATHER.
PORTUGUESE. LATTER PART OF SEVENTEENTH CENTURY.
(*Victoria and Albert Museum.*)

with the furniture, the old Chinese symbol of a dragon's foot holding a pearl, was repeated in the furniture by Dutch cabinetmakers. Dutch marquetry made an early appearance with simple ornamentation, sometimes enriched by ivory or mother-of-pearl inlay, but later it developed into flowing floral designs with figures, vases, fruit, butterflies, and elaborate scrolls in various coloured woods, of which yellow was the predominant colour.

SALE PRICES.

£ s. d

Charles II. Large Mirror, in walnut frame, finely inlaid with vases and sprays of flowers in marquetry, in shaped panels on wood of a darker colour, 45½ in. by 34½ in.   Puttick & Simpson, June 4, 1920 . . 89 5 0

Charles II. Casket, entirely covered with embroidery, worked with landscapes and figures in coloured silks, containing a tray, glass ink-bottles, &c., 11¼ in. wide. Christie, July 5, 1920 . . . . 32 11 0

Charles II. Casket, entirely covered with embroidery, worked with a king and other figures, animals and flowers in coloured silks, enriched with seed-pearls and coral, containing glass scent-bottles, &c., and mounted with silver handles and feet, 13 in. wide. Christie, July 5, 1920 . . . . . . 99 15 0

Marqueterie Cabinet, Charles II., elaborately inlaid with bird and flower decorations in various coloured woods and in ivory (6 ft. by 4 ft.). Sir Edward Holden Sale. Christie, March 24, 1920 . . . . 997 10 0

	£	s.	d.

Wardrobe, *en suite*, decorated in similar style (7 ft. by 6 ft.) from the Kent Gallery. Christie, March 24, 1920   357   0   0

Walnut Chest of Five Drawers, with panels of laburnum, the sides and top inlaid with circles, on stand with four drawers, cabriole legs and club feet, 40 in. wide. Puttick & Simpson, June 4, 1920 . .   81   18   0

James II. Oak Oblong Stool, on baluster turned legs and cross stretcher, $19\frac{1}{2}$ in. wide. Puttick & Simpson, May 28, 1920   29   8   0

James II. Oak Elbow Chair, the high back with shaped top, pierced and carved with foliage scrolls, and with extending elbows, the front rail also of scroll form, and with shaped legs and stretcher, the latter with vase centre, lined cane. Puttick & Simpson, May 28, 1920 .   31   10   0

Pair of William III. Walnut Armchairs, of unusual design, with scroll arms and tops, the seats and backs stuffed, and entirely covered with crimson velvet mounted with bands of amber velvet and gold braid, and the borders studded with brass bosses, on walnut rectangular legs with scroll feet, partly gilt. Property of Duke of Leeds. Christie, June 10, 1920 . . . . 819 0 0

Suite of William III. Furniture, the seats and backs stuffed, and covered with green and gold velvet, with scroll arms, turned legs, and X-shaped stretchers, the whole frameworks being coloured black, consisting of a settee, 34 in. wide, seven armchairs. Property of Duke of Leeds. Christie, June 10, 1920 . . . . . . 2835 0 0

William III. Settee, the seat, back, ends and loose cushions stuffed, and covered with Genoa velvet, with floral designs in colours on gold ground, the frameworks decorated with foliage in plasterwork, partly gilt and painted black, the back surmounted by three shields with coronet and monogram D.C.L. (presumably that of the first Duke of Leeds, who was created Earl of Danby, 1674, Marquis of Carmarthen, April 1694, and Duke of Leeds, May 1694), with X-shaped stretcher decorated with gadrooning, 7 ft. wide. Property of Duke of Leeds. Christie, June 10, 1920 . . . . . 1596 0 0

Day-bed, *en suite*, 5 ft. 3 in. long. £ s. d.
    Christie, June 10, 1920 . . . 1869 0 0
Pair of William and Mary Oak Chairs,
    the high backs with shaped and
    moulded borders, on scroll legs, the
    open front rails terminating with
    foliage scrolls, lined cane, the loose
    seats covered with old English
    needlework, designed with pastoral
    scenes with figures, sheep and
    poultry in panels, with scroll bor-
    ders on red ground, with flowers
    and foliage. Puttick & Simpson,
    June 4, 1920 . . . . . 94 10 0
William and Mary Mirror, in walnut
    marquetry frame, inlaid with run-
    ning flower and scroll ornament in
    different woods, 42 in. by 36 in.
    Puttick & Simpson, June 4, 1920 . 44 2 0
Walnut Chest of Five Drawers, with
    triple arcaded and moulded cornice,
    on stand, with shaped front and
    sides, spirally turned legs and
    stretcher, 43 in. wide. Puttick &
    Simpson, June 25, 1920 . . . 44 2 0

V

QUEEN ANNE
AND EARLY
GEORGIAN STYLES

QUEEN ANNE (1702–1714)

GEORGE I. (1714–1727)

GEORGE II. (1727–1760)

Queen Anne Walnut Chair with panelled cane back.

QUEEN ANNE OAK SETTLE.

Scrolled arms, panelled back and loose cushioned seat.
Width 6 feet.

V

QUEEN ANNE STYLE

Anne . . . . 1702–1714.	**1707.** Act of Union between England and Scotland. First United Parliament of Great Britain met.	
	1713. The National Debt had risen to £38,000,000.	

WITH the age of Queen Anne domestic furniture departed from the ornate characteristics which had marked previous epochs. The tendency in English furniture seems to have made towards comfort and homeliness. The English home may not have contained so many articles of luxury then as does the modern house with its artistic embellishments, and a popular taste rapidly ripening into a genuine love of the fine arts. " A modern shopkeeper's house," says Lord Macaulay, " is as well furnished as the house of a considerable merchant in Anne's reign." It is very doubtful whether this statement holds good with regard to the days of Elizabeth or the days of the early Stuarts, but there certainly seems to have been in the dawn of the walnut period a curtailment of luxurious effects that might well tempt a casual observer to generalise in the belief that the days of Anne spelt dulness in art.

The settle, the illustration of which is given (p. 149), bearing the date 1705, the year after Blenheim, shows that Jacobean models of early days were not forgotten. The inlaid borders are very effective, and there is nothing vulgar or offensive in the carving. It is simple in style and the joinery is good. A walnut mirror, carved and gilded (illustrated p. 137), exhibits the same solidity. There is nothing to show that the glorious age of Louis XIV. had produced the most sumptuous and richly decorated furniture the modern world had seen. The simplicity of this carved mirror frame is as though art had begun and ended in England, and probably it is this insularity of the furniture of this period, and the almost stubborn neglect of the important movements going on in France that makes the Queen Anne style of peculiar interest.

The oak desk illustrated (p. 139), dated 1696, is similar to the one at Abbotsford, in which Sir Walter

QUEEN ANNE MIRROR FRAME.
WALNUT, CARVED AND GILDED.

Scott mislaid his manuscript of "Waverley," where it lay among his fishing-tackle for eleven years.

Another piece of the same period is the cupboard with carved doors and drawers beneath (illustrated p. 140).

OAK DESK.

WITH INITIALS "L. G." AND DATED 1696.

(From the collection of T. E. Price Stretche, Esq.)

Some pretty effects were now obtained by veneering, which was largely coming into practice. The pieces with the burr-walnut panels, marked in a series of knot-like rings, are especially sought after. This pattern was obtained from the gnarled roots of the

By permission of
T. B. Price Stretche, Esq.

OAK CUPBOARD.   SEVENTEENTH CENTURY.

Metal handles of drawers, eighteenth century.

(Height 6 ft. 7 in. ; width, 4 ft. 6 in.)

walnut-tree, and applied in a decorative manner with
excellent result.

CHEST OF DRAWERS.   VENEERED IN WALNUT.

On turned legs ; with original metal escutcheons and handles.

Typical of early eighteenth century reticent cabinet work, the prototype of later
English styles.

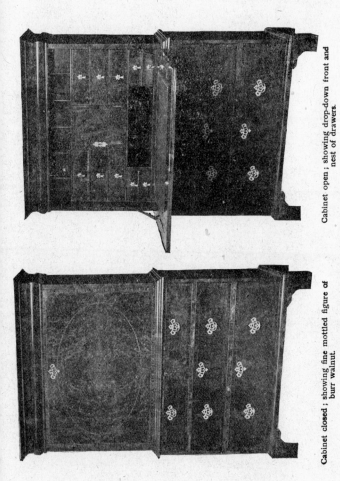

Cabinet closed; showing fine mottled figure of burr walnut.

Cabinet open; showing drop-down front and nest of drawers.

QUEEN ANNE WALNUT CABINET.

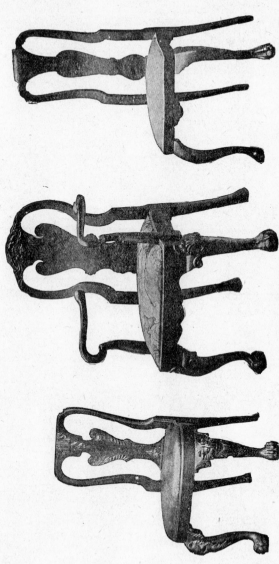

Walnut chair with fiddle-shaped splat, cabriole legs, claw and ball feet.

Walnut armchair with fiddle-shaped splat, cabriole legs and claw and ball feet.

Chair, decorated in black and gold lac, with urn splat, cabriole legs, and claw and ball feet.

CHAIRS : QUEEN ANNE AND EARLY GEORGIAN PERIOD.

In the fine cabinet, the illustration of which is given (p. 141), the style is typical of this period. The panels of the doors are of exquisite finish, and show a beautiful walnut grain of peculiarly-pleasing mottled appearance, and the mellow effect which time has given to this specimen cannot be imitated with any degree of success in modern replicas. In the illustration showing this piece when open, the rich effect of the walnut in the middle panel may be noticed ; the contemporary brass handles to the nest of drawers are typical of this style.

In chairs and in tables the elegant cabriole and colt's-foot legs were now commonly adopted, and apparently, simple as is the construction, it is only when Queen Anne pieces come to be repaired that it is found how expensive an undertaking it is, owing to their ingenious construction and the patient labour that was expended upon them, to produce unpretentious and harmonious effects.

The assertively English spirit which was the dominant note of the furniture of the early eighteenth century continued up till the early years of the reign of George II. During this period, which covers half a century, walnut was the wood mostly used in the manufacture of furniture, and this walnut period shows a quiet dignity of style and a simple proportion, reticently elegant and inornate without being severe.

The Queen Anne oak settle, with shaped panelled back and scroll arms, which appears as the headpiece to this chapter, is especially representative of the kind of piece in common use at the time ; oak was still employed in furniture of this nature. The legs show the newer design, which was already departing from the elegant turning of earlier Jacobean days.

In the Queen Anne chair which is illustrated in the group of chairs of this period (p. 143), with open back and carved scroll foliage, the cabriole legs are finely carved with lion masks and acanthus leaf ornament, on lion's claw-and-ball feet. The seat is removable, and is stuffed. Queen Anne chairs had high carved or plain splat backs. The armchair in the same group shows this type of back. The Dutch shell-pattern often appears either on back or at the juncture of the leg with the seat. Chairs decorated in marquetry, in Dutch fashion, were in use at this period. The one illustrated with the two above-mentioned chairs is inlaid with birds and flowers, and the legs are cabriole. The seat follows the growing usage of being loose and stuffed.

Dutch marquetry cabinets on stands, with straight uprights, were imported and became a feature in the early eighteenth century drawing-room (see illustration, p. 147). The earlier forms had straight sides, but later, as the fashion grew, bureaux and large cabinets, with the dimensions of a modern wardrobe, had taken their place, with *bombé* or swelled sides, and profusely decorated in marquetry, with vases and tulips and unnamed flowers of the cabinet-maker's invention, birds, butterflies, and elaborate scrollwork, in which ivory and mother-of-pearl were often employed as an inlay.

The stands on which the smaller cabinets stood were turned with the spiral leg of Jacobean days, and later they have the cabriole leg, with ball-and-claw or club feet. Cabinets and stands are frequently found together, in which the one is much earlier than the other.

Rich damask began to be used in the furnishing of hangings, and in some of the palatial furniture of the period the looms of Spitalfields produced the coverings. In Queen Anne's bedroom the hangings were of rich silk velvet.

Clocks of the variety termed "Grandfather," either with fine walnut cases or inlaid with marquetry, came into more general use in the days of Queen Anne. An elaboration of carving

By permission of Messrs. Hampton & Sons

DUTCH MARQUETRY CABINET.

Fitted with shelves. Door richly inlaid with flowers and scrolled foliage. On stand with turned legs and stretcher.

QUEEN ANNE CLOCK.
Walnut case with marquetry work.

on grandfather clock cases as a rule is to be regarded with suspicion. Plain panels are not so saleable as carved ones; the want is supplied, and many fine old clock cases are spoiled by having the touch of a modern hand. The clock illustrated is an untouched specimen. The walnut case is a fine example of Queen Anne marquetry work. The works are by Sam Barrow, Hermitage Bridge, London. The steel dial is richly mounted with cupids, masks, and scrolls in chased brass.

Towards the middle of the eighteenth century and later, cabinets of Dutch importation, and Japanese or Chinese in origin, were extensively in use. In smaller numbers they had, without doubt, in the days of William and Mary, been introduced, but it was not until the commerce with the East had been well established that they became popular. In the cabinet illustrated (p. 150)

WILLIAM AND MARY CHEST OF DRAWERS.

On original stand. Decorated in marquetry. Side showing panel in common use by
cabinet-makers and clock-case makers.

(By courtesy of Messrs. Hampton & Son.)

CHEST OF DRAWERS, DECORATED IN MARQUETRY.

Side showing panel in common use by cabinet-makers and clock-case makers.

(By courtesy of Messrs. A. B. Daniell & Sons.)

the cabinet-work is English, the drawers are all dovetailed in the English manner, but the lacquered doors come from the East. It is an especially

QUEEN ANNE OAK SETTLE. DATED 1705.

With borders in marquetry.

(Width, 5 ft.)

interesting example, as the pagoda-like super-structure is not often found complete.

Lacquered boxes had been sent home from the

11

East by English, French, and Dutch merchants, for many years, and with characteristic ingenuity the

OLD LAC CABINET.
ENGLISH; EARLY EIGHTEENTH CENTURY.

French cabinetmakers had employed these as panels for their furniture, but the supply not being sufficient they had attempted a lacquer of their own, which is

dealt with in a subsequent chapter on Louis XIV.
furniture.   Dutch lacquer-work was a similar attempt

LAC CABINET.   MIDDLE OF EIGHTEENTH CENTURY.

(Height, 2 ft. 5 in. ; width, 2 ft. 8½ in. ; depth, 1 ft. 6½ in. ; height of stand, 2 ft. 9 in.

(From the collection of W. G. Honey, Esq., Cork.)

on the part of the craftsman of Holland to equal the
Oriental originals.

In the early eighteenth century the English craftsman tried his skill at lacquered furniture, it is true
not with very successful results, but it is interesting
to see what he has left as attempts. The illustration
(p. 143) of a chair in black and gold lac is of English
manufacture. The splat back and the cabriole leg
give the date, and the specimen is a noteworthy
example. Another piece of the first half of the

W. G. Honey, Esq., Cork.

FRONT OF LAC CABINET (ILLUSTRATED),
WITH DOORS CLOSED.

eighteenth cen-
tury period is the
lac cabinet illus-
trated (p. 151).
The metal hinges
and corners of
this are of chased
brass and of Eng-
lish or Dutch
workmanship.
The shape and
design of the
drawer handles
are frequently
found in nests of
drawers of this period, and there was a singular fondness shown at this time for numbers of small drawers
and pigeon-holes in furniture. The now familiar
bureau with bookcase above, and drop-down, sloping
front covering drawers and recesses, dates from this
time. The escutcheon of the lac cabinet is illustrated
in detail as a tailpiece to this chapter to show the
particular style of work found on the locks and hinges
and drawer-handles of pieces of this nature. As has

been said before, it is especially useful to the collector to make himself thoroughly familiar with these details of the various periods.

It may be readily imagined that at a time when cards were the passion of everybody in society, the card-table became a necessary piece of furniture in eighteenth-century days, just before the dawn of the great age of mahogany, when Chippendale, and the school that followed him, eagerly worked in the wood which Raleigh discovered. They produced countless forms, both original and adapted from the French, which have enriched the *répertoire* of the cabinet-maker and which have brought fame to the man whose designs added lustre to the reputation of English furniture.

SALE PRICES.

	£	s.	d.

Armchair, Queen Anne, large walnut wood, carved with foliage, the arms terminating in masks, on carved cabriole legs and lion's-claw feet. Christie, March 29, 1904 . . .   50   8   o

Cabinet, Queen Anne, the lower part fitted with escritoire, the upper part with numerous drawers, shaped cornice above, 3 ft. 6 in. by 7 ft. 6 in. Puttick & Simpson, April 12, 1904   34   0   0

Chairs, four Queen Anne, walnut wood, with interlaced backs carved with rosettes and a shell at the top, on cabriole legs carved with shells and foliage, and a pair of chairs made to match. Christie, July 8, 1904   44   2   0

Walnut Chest of Five Drawers, the panels of laburnum inlaid with hexafoil and scroll ornament in holly, 36 in. wide. Puttick & Simpson, June 4, 1920 . . .   73   10   0

Pair of Walnut Chairs, the shaped high backs with moulded borders, surmounted by pierced and carved foliage ornament the centres inlaid

£   s.   d.

with flowers in quatrefoil panels of
a lighter wood, on square cabriole
legs and turned stretchers, lined
cane. Puttick & Simpson, June 4,
1920   48   6   0

Queen Anne Double Chest of Ten
Drawers of Tortoiseshell Lacquer,
the front with four vertical recesses
having arcaded tops, painted and
gilt with Chinese garden scenes
and figures, animals, birds and
flowers in panels, and with shaped
and moulded borders, the sides gilt
with storks and bamboo, 39½ in.
wide. Puttick & Simpson, June 25,
1920   126   0   0

Queen Anne Red Lacquer Cabinet, with
folding doors enclosing drawers,
the whole decorated with Chinese
landscapes in gold and silver on
red ground, mounted with en-
graved metal-gilt hinges, on stand
carved with a female mask and
decorated with foliage in gold on
red ground, 5 ft. high, 35 in.
wide. Property of Duke of Leeds.
Christie, June 10, 1920 . . .   2331   0   0

Walnut Folding Card Table, of quatrefoil form, with shaped and inlaid
borders, outlined with holly, and

	£	s.	d.
with drawer, on baluster turned legs and shaped stretchers, 34½ in. wide. Puttick & Simpson, June 25, 1920	33	12	0
Queen Anne Mirror, in walnut frame, with carved gilt foliage borders and scroll top, 60 in. high, 30 in. wide. Christie, July 14, 1920 . . .	42	0	0
Queen Anne Mirror, in walnut frame, the scroll outline carved and gilt with foliage, the pediment with shell centre, 35½ in. by 36 in. Puttick & Simpson, June 4, 1920 .	18	18	0
Queen Anne Mirror, with two plates, in gilt wood frame, carved with animals, flowers and scrolls, the shaped top with foliage and shell ornament, 66½ in. by 25 in. Puttick & Simpson, June 4, 1920 .	31	10	0

VI

FRENCH FURNITURE.
THE PERIOD OF
LOUIS XIV

(1643–1715).

CONTEMPORARY WITH CHARLES I., THE
COMMONWEALTH, CHARLES II., JAMES II.,
WILLIAM AND MARY AND QUEEN ANNE

CASSETTE. FRENCH; SEVENTEENTH CENTURY.

Containing many secret drawers.

VI

FRENCH FURNITURE. THE PERIOD OF LOUIS XIV

Louis XIV. (1643–1715), covering English periods of Civil War, Commonwealth, Charles II., James II., William and Mary, and Anne.

1619–1683. Colbert, Minister of Finance and patron of the arts.

1661–1687. Versailles built.

1662. Gobelins Tapestry Works started by Colbert; Le Brun first director (1662–1690).

1664. Royal Academy of Painting, Architecture, and Sculpture founded by Colbert, to which designs of furniture were admitted.

IN order to arrive at a sense of proportion as to the value of English furniture and its relation to contemporary art in Europe, it is necessary to pass under hasty examination the movements that were taking place in France in the creation of a new style in furniture under the impulses of the epoch of the *Grande Monarque*. To estimate more correctly the styles of the Early Jacobean and of the later English furniture extending to the days of Chippendale and Sheraton, it must be borne in mind that England was not always so insular in art as the days of Queen Anne would seem to indicate. It is impossible for the cabinetmakers and the craftsmen to have utterly ignored the splendours of France. Louis XIV. had a long and eventful reign, which extended from the days when Charles I. was marshalling his forces to engage in civil war with the Parliament down to the closing years of Queen Anne. During his minority it cannot be said that Louis XIV. influenced art in furniture, but from 1661, contemporary with Charles II., when he assumed the despotic power that he exercised for half a century, his love of sumptuousness, and his personal supervision of the etiquette of a formal Court, in which no detail was omitted to surround royalty with magnificence, made him the patron of the fine arts, and gave his Court the most splendid prestige in Europe.

As a headpiece to this chapter we give a very fine example of a *cassette*, or strong box, of the time of Louis XIV. It is securely bound with metal bands of exquisite design. The interior is fitted with a number of secret drawers.

In the illustration (p. 159) it will be seen that the chair of the period of Louis Treize differed in no great respects from the furniture under the early Stuarts in

this country. This design is by the celebrated Crispin
de Passe, and the date is when Charles I. raised his
standard at Nottingham, a year prior to the birth of
Louis XIV.

During the reign of Louis XIV.,
tables, armoires, and cabinets were
designed on architectural princi-
ples.   Under the guiding influence
of Colbert, Minister of Finance,
architects and cabinetmakers were
selected to design furniture for the
Tuileries, the Louvre, and Fontainebleau.   In the
early years of the
reign furniture was
made with severe
lines, but gradually
it became the prac-
tice to fashion larger
pieces.   Immense
tables with sumptu-
ous decoration, on
gilded claw feet, and
having tops inlaid
with *pietra-dura* in-
tended to carry
bronze groups and
porphyry vases,
were made at the

CHAIR OF PERIOD OF LOUIS XIII.
DESIGNED BY CRISPIN DE PASSE, 1642.

Gobelins factory, under the direction of the celebrated
Le Brun. This artist loved grandeur and gorgeousness in decoration, and in accord with the personal

ideas of Louis XIV., who had an inordinate love for perfect symmetry, huge pieces of furniture were built in magnificent manner to please the taste of the *Grande Monarque*.   Men of genius were employed in the manufacture of tapestries, of furniture, and of metal mountings, and the interior decorations of the palaces were designed in harmony with the furniture intended for use therein.

The most illustrious among the cabinetmakers was André Charles Boule, who was made, in 1673, by letters patent, *Premier ébéniste de la maison royale*. The work of this artist in wood has attained a world-wide celebrity, and his name even has been corrupted into "buhl" to denote a particular class of work which he perfected.   His most notable productions are the finely chased ormolu, in which he was an accomplished worker, and the inlay of tortoiseshell and brass, sometimes varied with ebony or silver, which have remained the wonder of succeeding generations.

Boule was born in 1642, and lived till 1732.   The first Boule, termed " *Le Père*," he was succeeded by no less than four sons and nephews of the same name, in addition to his pupils who carried on his traditions at the Boule *atelier*, and a crowd of later imitators, even up to the present day, have followed his style in lavish decoration without being possessed of his skill.

In Italy and in France marquetry of considerable delicacy and of fine effect had been produced long before the epoch of Louis XIV., but it was Boule who introduced a novelty into marquetry by his veneered work, which rapidly grew into favour till it

developed into cruder colouring in inlays and un-
bridled licence in ornamentation, to which its origi-
nator would never have given countenance.

The pieces of furniture usually associated with him
are massive structures of ebony with their surfaces
covered with tortoiseshell, in which are inlaid
arabesques, scrolls, and foliage in thin brass or other
metal. Upon the surface of this metal inlay further
ornamentation was chased with the burin. This
alternation of tortoiseshell and brass forms a brilliant
marquetry. Into the chased designs on the metal a
black enamel was introduced to heighten the effect,
which was further increased by portions of the wood
beneath the semi-transparent tortoiseshell being
coloured black or brown or red ; sometimes a bluish-
green was used. Later imitators, not content with the
beautiful effect of tortoiseshell, used horn in parts,
which is more transparent, and they did not fear the
garish effect of blue or vermilion underneath. Boule's
creations, set in massive mounts and adornments of
masks and bas-reliefs, cast in gilt-bronze and chased,
were pieces of furniture of unsurpassed magnificence,
and especially designed for the mirrored splendours
of the *salons* of Versailles.

In boule-work all parts of the marquetry are held
down by glue to the bed, usually of oak, the metal
being occasionally fastened down by small brass
pins, which are hammered flat and chased over so
as to be imperceptible.

In order to economise the material, Boule, when
his marquetry became in demand, employed a process
which led to the use of the technical terms, *boule* and

counter-boule.   The brass and the tortoiseshell were cut into thin sheets.   A number of sheets of brass were clamped together with the same number of sheets of tortoiseshell.   The design was then cut out, the result being that each sheet of tortoiseshell had a design cut out of it, into which the same design from one of the sheets of brass would exactly fit. Similarly each sheet of brass had a design cut out of it into which a corresponding piece of tortoiseshell would fit. That in which the ground is of tortoiseshell and the inlaid portion is brass, is considered the better, and is called *boule*, or the *première partie*.   That in which the groundwork is brass and the design inlaid is of tortoiseshell, is called *counter-boule* or *contre-partie*. This latter is used for side panels.

An examination of the specimens preserved in the Louvre, at the Jones Bequest at the Victoria and Albert Museum, or in the Wallace Collection will enable the student to see more readily how this practice works out in the finished result.   In the illustration (p. 163) of the two pedestals the effect of the employment of *boule* and *counter-boule* is shown.

Associated with Boule is Jean Bérain, who had a fondness for the Italian style; his designs are more symmetrically correct, both in ornamental detail and in architectural proportion.   His conceptions are remarkable for their fanciful elaboration, and their wealth of profuse scrollwork.   In the French national collections at the Louvre, at Versailles, and elsewhere there are many beautiful examples of his chandeliers of magnificent carved and gilded work.   The freedom of the spiral arms and complex coils he introduced

PEDESTALS SHOWING BOULE AND COUNTER-BOULE WORK

(*Wallace Collection.*)

(*a*) Boule or   (*b*) Counter-boule or
première partie.   *contre-partie.*

into his candelabra have never been equalled as harmonious portions of a grandly conceived scheme of magnificent interior decoration, to which, in the days

BOULE CABINET, OR ARMOIRE.
Valued at nearly £15,000.
(*Victoria and Albert Museum.*)

of Louis XIV., so much artistic talent was devoted. With regard to the value of some of the specimens in the national collections, it is difficult to form an estimate. The Boule cabinet, probably designed by Bérain, executed by Boule for Louis XIV. (illustrated p. 165) would, if put up for sale at Christie's, probably fetch £15,000. This piece is held to be grander in style than any in the galleries in France. At the Wallace Collection there are examples which would bring fabulous sums if sold. A cabinet by Boule, in the Jones Bequest, purchased by Mr. Jones for £3,000 in 1881, is now worth three times that sum.

Upon the building, decorating, and furnishing of Versailles Louis XIV. spent over five hundred million francs, in addition to which there was the army of workmen liable to statute labour. Some twenty thousand men and six thousand horses were employed in 1684 at the different parts of the château and park. In May, 1685, there were no less than thirty-six thousand employed.

The illustrious craftsmen who were employed upon the magnificent artistic interior decorations have transmitted their names to posterity. Bérain, Lepautre, Henri de Gissey, are the best known of the designers. Among the painters are the names of Audran, Baptiste, Jouvenet, Mignard, and the best known of the sculptors are Coustou and Van Clève. Of the woodcarvers, metal-chasers, locksmiths, and gilders Pierre Taupin, Ambroise Duval, Delobel, and Goy are names of specialists in their own craft who transformed Versailles from a royal hunting-box into one of the most splendid palaces in Europe.

SALE PRICES.

£ s. d.

Commode, Louis XIV., of inlaid king-
wood, with two drawers, mounted
with handles and masks at the
corners of chased ormolu, and surmounted by a fleur violette marble
slab, 52 in. wide. Christie, January
22, 1904 . . . .   31 10 0

Show-cabinet, of Louis XIV. design,
inlaid king-wood, with glazed folding doors, ormolu mounts, chased
and surmounted by vases, 73 in.
high, 46 in. wide.   Christie, April
12, 1904 . . . . . .   30 9 0

Casket, Louis XIV., black Boule, inlaid
with Cupids, vases of flowers and
scrolls, and fitted with four tortoiseshell and gold picqué shell-shaped
snuff boxes. Christie, April 19, 1904.   73 10 0

Commode, Louis XIV., Boule, of sarco-
phagus form, containing two drawers, at either corners are detached
cabriole legs, the various panels
are inlaid with brass and tortoiseshell, the whole is mounted with
ormolu, surmounted by a slab of
veined marble, 49 in. wide. Christie,
May 27, 1904 . . . . . .   57 15 0

VII

FRENCH FURNITURE
THE PERIOD OF
LOUIS XV

(1715–1774)

CONTEMPORARY WITH GEORGE I.,
GEORGE II., AND GEORGE III.

COMMODE, BY CRESSENT.

(From a drawing by Walter Eassie.

(*Wallace Collection.*)

VII

FRENCH FURNITURE. THE PERIOD OF LOUIS XV

Louis XV. . . . 1715–1774.	Petit Trianon built at Versailles. Meissonier, Director of Royal Factories (1723–1774). Watteau (1684–1721). Pater (1695–1736). Lancret (1690–1743). Boucher (1704–1770). **1751.** The leading *ébénistes* compelled to stamp their work with their names.

LOUIS XIV. died in the year following the death of Queen Anne, so that it will be readily seen that

English art was uninfluenced by France in the days of William and Mary, and how insular it had become under Anne. The English craftsman was not fired by new impulses from France during such an outburst of decorative splendour. The reign of Louis XV. extends from George I. down to the eleventh year of the reign of George III., which year saw the cargoes of tea flung into Boston harbour and the beginning of the war with America.

In glancing at the Louis Quinze style it will be observed how readily it departed from the studied magnificence of Louis XIV. In attempting elegance of construction and the elimination of much that was massive and cumbersome in the former style, it developed in its later days into meaningless ornament and trivial construction. At first it possessed considerable grace, but towards the end of the reign the designs ran riot in rococo details, displaying incongruous decoration.

It was the age of the elegant boudoir, and the bedroom became a place for more intimate guests than those received in the large reception-room. In the days of Louis XIV. the bed was a massive structure, but in the succeeding reign it became an elegant appendage to a room. At Versailles the splendid galleries of magnificent proportion were transformed by the Duke of Orleans, Regent of France (1715–1723) during the king's minority, into smaller *salons* covered in wainscoting, painted white and ornamented with gilded statues. In like manner the Louis Quinze decorations were ruthlessly destroyed by Louis-Philippe.

By permission of Messrs. Waring.

LOUIS XV. PARQUETERY COMMODE.

With chased and bronze-gilt mounts.

(Formerly in the Hamilton Palace Collection.)

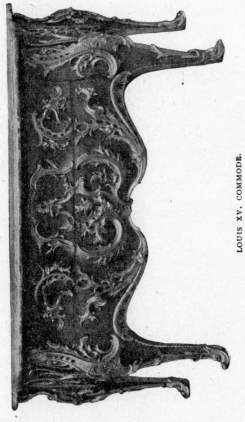

LOUIS XV. COMMODE.

BY CAFFIERI.

The commode in the Wallace Collection (illustrated p. 171) is of the time when Louis XV. was in his minority, and of the days of the Regency. It is by Charles Cressent (1685–1768), who was cabinetmaker to Philippe d'Orleans, Regent of France. This is an especially typical specimen of the class to which it belongs as showing the transition style between Louis XIV. and the succeeding reign.

To establish Louis the Fifteenth's *petits apparte-ments* the gallery painted by Mignard was demolished, and later, in 1752, the Ambassadors' Staircase was destroyed, the masterpiece of the architects Levau and Dorbay, and the marvel of Louis the Fourteenth's Versailles.

It is necessary to bear these facts in mind in order to see how a new French monarch set ruthlessly new fashions in furniture and created a taste for his personal style in art. In the first part of the Louis Quinze period the metal mountings by Caffieri and Cressent are of exquisite style ; they are always of excellent workmanship, but later they betrayed the tendency of the time for fantastic curves, which had affected the furniture to such an extent that no straight lines were employed, and the sides of com-modes and other pieces were swelled into unwieldy proportions, and instead of symmetrical and har-monious results the florid style, known as the " rococo," choked all that was beautiful in design. Meissonier, Director of the Royal Factories (1723–1774), was mainly responsible for this unnatural development. He revelled in elaborate combinations of shellwork and impossible foliage.

In the Louis XV. commodes illustrated (pp. 173, 175) it will be seen how far superior is the design and treatment of the one which was formerly in the celebrated Hamilton Collection. Its chased and gilt mounts are harmoniously arranged, and though the ornamentation is superbly rich, it breaks no canons of art by overloaded detail or coarse profusion. Not so much can be said for the other commode of the rococo style, even though the mounts be by Caffieri and executed in masterly manner. There is a wanton abandonment and an offensive tone in the florid treatment which point clearly to the decline of taste in art.

The highest art of concealment was not a prominent feature in a Court which adopted its style from the caprices of Madame du Pompadour or the whims of Madame du Barry. But among the finest productions are the splendid pieces of reticent cabinet-making by the celebrated Jean François Oeben, who came from Holland. His preference was for geometrical patterns, varied only with the sparing use of flowers, in producing his most delicate marquetry. In the pieces by Boule and others, not in tortoise-shell but in wood inlay, the wood was so displayed as to exhibit in the panels the grain radiating from the centre. Oeben did not forget this principle, and placed his bouquets of flowers, when, on occasion, he used them, in the centre of his panels, and filled up the panel with geometric design.

The well-known maker, Charles Cressent (1685–1768), used rosewood, violet, and amaranth woods in his marquetry, and at this time many new foreign woods were employed by the cabinetmakers in France and Italy. In addition to woods of a natural colour, it was the practice artificially to colour light woods.

LOUIS XV. *ESCRITOIRE À TOILETTE.*

Of tulip-wood and sycamore, inlaid with landscapes in coloured woods

Formerly in the possession of Queen Marie Antoinette

(*Jones Bequest: Victoria and Albert Museum.*)

and inlay work was attempted in which trophies of war, musical instruments, or the shepherd's crook hung with ribbon, were all worked out in marquetry. Pictures, in coloured woods, in imitation of oil paintings on canvas, were foolishly attempted, and altogether the art of inlay, ingenious and wonderful in its construction, began to affect trivialities and surprising effects most unsuited to the range of its technique.

In the toilet-table illustrated (p. 179), this misapplication of inlay to reproduce pictures is seen on the three front panels and on the middle panel above. The chief woods employed are tulip and sycamore, inlaid with tinted lime, holly, and cherry-woods. The mountings of the table are chased ormolu. The cylindrical front encloses drawers with inlaid fronts. Beneath this is a sliding shelf, under which is a drawer with three compartments, fitted with toilet requisites and having inlaid lids. This specimen of Louis Quinze work is in the Jones Collection at the Victoria and Albert Museum. It was formerly in the possession of Queen Marie Antoinette. It is attributed to Oeben, though from comparison with some of the chaster work known to have come from his hand it would seem to be of too fanciful marquetry for his restrained and sober style.

It is especially true of the furniture of this great French period that it requires harmonious surroundings The slightest false touch throws everything out of balance at once. Of this fact the inventors were well aware. If Dutch furniture requires the quiet, restful art of Cuyp or Van der Neer, or Metzu or Jan Steen on the surrounding walls, the interiors of Louis Quinze demand the works of contemporary French genre-painters.

All things worked together to produce a harmonious *ensemble* in this brilliant period. The royal tapestry and Sèvres porcelain factories turned out their most beautiful productions to decorate rooms, furniture,

LOUIS XV. SECRÉTAIRE.

By Riesener, in his earlier manner.

IN TRANSITIONAL STYLE, APPROACHING LOUIS
SEIZE PERIOD.

(*Wallace Collection.*)

and for the table. Tapestries from Beauvais, Gobelins, and Aubusson, rich silks from the looms of Lyons, or from Lucca, Genoa, or Venice were made for wall-hangings, for chair-backs, for seats, and for sofas.

Fragonard, Natoire, and Boucher painted lunettes over chimney-fronts, or panels of ceilings. Of great cabinetmakers, Riesener and David Roentgen, princes among *ébénistes*, worked in wonderful manner in tulip-wood, in holly, in rosewood, purple wood, and laburnum to produce marquetry, the like of which has never been seen before nor since.

Associated with the period of Louis XV. is the love for the lacquered panel. Huygens, a Dutchman, had achieved good results in imitations of Oriental lacquer, which in France, under the hand of Martin, a carriage-painter, born about 1706, rivalled the importations from Japan. It is stated that the secret of the fine, transparent lac polish that he used was obtained from the missionaries who resided in Japan before the date of the massacres and foreign expulsion of all except the Dutch traders. Vernis-Martin, as his varnish was termed, became in general request. From 1744 for twenty years, Sieur Simon Etienne Martin was granted a monopoly to manufacture this lacquered work in the Oriental style. Although he declared that his secret would die with him, other members of his family continued the style, which was taken up by many imitators in the next reign. His varnish had a peculiar limpid transparency, and he obtained the wavy network of gold groundwork so successfully produced by Japanese and Chinese craftsmen. On this were delicately painted, by Boucher and other artists, Arcadian subjects, framed in rocaille style with gold thickly laid on, and so pure that in the bronze gilding and in the woodwork it maintains its fine lustre to the present day.

THE "BUREAU DU ROI."

THE MASTERPIECE OF RIESENER.

(From a drawing by Walter Eassie.)

(*Wallace Collection.*)

Towards the close of the reign of Louis XV. a new style set in, which reverted to simpler tastes, to which the name "*À la reine*" was given, in deference to the taste which is supposed to have emanated from Marie Leczinska, the queen, but is said to have been due to Madame du Pompadour.

At the Wallace Collection is a fine secrétaire, with the mounts and ornaments of gilt bronze cast and chased, which is illustrated (p. 181). The central panel of marquetry shows, in life size, a cock, with the caducens, a snake, a banner, and symbolical instruments. It is by Jean François Riesener, and in his earliest manner, made in the later years of Louis Quinze in the Transitional style approaching the Louis Seize period.

Among the wonderful creations of Riesener, probably his masterpiece is the celebrated "Bureau du Roi," begun in 1760 by Oeben, and completed in 1769 by Riesener—who married the widow of Oeben, by the way. Its bronzes are by Duplesis, Winant, and Hervieux. The design and details show the transition between the Louis Quinze and the Louis Seize styles.

The original, which is at the Louvre, is in marquetry of various coloured woods and adorned by plaques of gilt bronze, cast and chased. The copy from which our illustration is taken (p. 183) is in the Wallace Collection, and is by Dasson, and follows the original in proportions, design, and technique.

SALE PRICES.

£   s.   d.

Table, Louis XV., oblong, the legs are
cabriole, it contains one drawer
and a writing-slide ; around the
sides are inlaid panels of old Japanese lacquer, each panel bordered
by elaborate scrollwork of chased
ormolu, signed with " B. V. R. B.,"
surmounted by a slab of white
marble, 39 in. wide. Christie,
December 18, 1903 . . . . 1900 0 0

Writing-table, Louis XV., marquetry,
with sliding top and drawer, fitted
with movable writing slab, com-
partment for ink-vases, &c., signed
" L. Doudin," Louis XV. form with
cabriole legs, the top decorated
with scrolls forming panels, the
centre one containing a Teniers
figure subject, parquetry and inlays
of flowers round the sides, corner
mounts, &c., of ormolu, cast and
chased, 30 in. wide. Christie, March
18, 1904 . . . . . . 630 0 0

Cartonnière, Louis XV., of inlaid tulip-
wood, containing a clock by Palan-
son, à Paris, mounted with
Chinese figures, masks, foliage and

	£	s.	d.

scrolls of chased ormolu, 48 in. high, 36 in. wide. Christie, April 22, 1904 . . . . 409 10 0

Louis XV. Small Marqueterie Escritoire, with sloping front and three drawers below, inlaid with branches of foliage on tulip- and king-wood ground, and mounted with ormolu, 32 in. wide. Christie, July 20, 1920 . . 27 8 0

Louis XV. Small Table, with three drawers, veneered with tulip- and king-wood and mounted with ormolu, the top covered with leather, 16 in. wide. Christie, July 20, 1920 94 10 0

Another, nearly similar, with marqueterie panels inlaid with branches of flowers, 16½ in. wide. Christie, July 20, 1920 . . . . . 100 16 0

Louis XV. Marqueterie Table of scroll outline with one drawer, the frieze and legs inlaid with festoons of flowers and foliage in king-wood on tulip-wood ground with king-wood borders ; mounted with ormolu borders and leg-mounts chased with acanthus foliage, beading and strapwork, the top covered with green velvet. From the Collection of the Earl of Essex. Arnold Sale. Christie, June 8, 1920 . . . 1837 10 0

£ s. d.

Pair of Louis XV. Small Tables, one fitted with a writing-slide and three drawers, and the other with two drawers, inlaid with branches of flowers on king-wood ground, and mounted with ormolu corners chased with foliage and scrolls, and surmounted by veined marble slabs, with brocade screens at the backs, 19 in. wide. Harland-Peck Sale. Christie, June 23, 1920 . 504 0 0

Louis XV. Upright Marqueterie Cabinet, enclosed by folding doors, inlaid with flowers in various woods and scrollwork in king-wood on tulip-wood ground, mounted with chased ormolu corners, and surmounted by a veined red marble slab, 28 in. wide, stamped " P. Roussel." Christie, July 8, 1920 . . . 141 15 0

Louis XV. Small Table. with writing-slide and one drawer, veneered with tulip-wood, and mounted with chased ormolu escutcheons and corners, 24 in. wide. Christie, July 8, 1920 . . . . . . 158 16 0

Louis XV. Writing-Table, veneered with tulip-wood and mounted with ormolu escutcheons and corners chased with busts. flowers and

scrollwork, the top covered with
green leather, 63 in. wide. Christie,
July 14, 1920 . . . . . 283 10 0

Louis XV. Small Marqueterie Secrétaire, with cylinder front and three
drawers below, inlaid with branches
of flowers and panels of cube-
pattern on tulip-wood ground, and
mounted with ormolu corners
chased with flowers and scrollwork,
32 in. wide. Christie, July 8, 1920 . 89 5 0

Louis XV. Parqueterie Writing-Table,
with a writing-slide and three
drawers, inlaid with panels of trelliswork in mahogany borders, mounted with ormolu escutcheons and
corners chased with foliage and
scrollwork, the top covered with
green leather, 37 in. wide. Christie,
July 8, 1920 . . . . . 105 0 0

VIII

FRENCH
FURNITURE.
THE PERIOD OF
LOUIS XVI
(1774–1793)

CONTEMPORARY WITH THE
REIGN OF GEORGE III.

VIII

FRENCH FURNITURE. THE PERIOD OF LOUIS XVI

Louis XVI. . . . 1774–1793.	**1730–1806.** Riesener, *ébéniste* to Marie Antoinette (born near Cologne).
	1789. Commencement of the French Revolution.

THE so-called Louis Seize period embraces much that is good from the later days of the previous reign. The same designers were employed with the addition of a few younger men. Caffieri and Riesener were producing excellent work, and above all was Gouthière, whose renown as a founder and chaser of gilded bronze ornaments is unrivalled. Elegance and simplicity are again the prevailing notes. Straight lines took the place of the twisted contortions of the rococo style. Thin scrolls, garlands, ribbons and knots, classical cameo-shaped panels, and Sèvres plaques form the characteristic ornamentation.

The acanthus-leaf, distorted into unnatural pro portions in the middle Louis Quinze period, returned to its normal shape, the egg-and-tongue moulding came into use, and the delicacy of the laurel-leaf was employed in design in Louis Seize decorations.

In the jewel cabinet illustrated (p. 193), the new style is shown at its best. The cabinet is inlaid in rosewood and sycamore, and bears the name of " J. H. Riesener " stamped on it. The chased ormolu mounts are by Gouthière. The geometrical inlay is a tradition which Oeben left to his successors. The upper portion has a rising lid with internal trays. In the lower part is a drawer and a shelf. This piece is at the Victoria and Albert Museum in the Jones Bequest, and it is well worth detailed examination as being a representative specimen of the most artistic work produced at this period.

Pierre Gouthière had a complete mastery over his technique. The estimation with which his work is regarded has made furniture which he mounted bring extraordinary prices. In 1882, at the dispersal of the celebrated Hamilton Palace Collection, three specimens with his workmanship realised £30,000.

The Vernis-Martin panels were decorated by Watteau and Pater. The age of artificialities with its *fêtes-galantes* in the royal gardens of the Luxembourg and in the pleasure parks of the Court, with the ill-starred Marie Antoinette playing at shepherds and shepherdesses, had its influence upon art. Watteau employed his brush to daintily paint the attitudes of *Le Lorgneur* upon a fan-mount, or to depict elegantly dressed noblemen and ladies of the Court dancing elaborate minuets in satin shoes, or feasting from exquisite Sèvres porcelain dishes in the damp corner of some park or old château.

LOUIS XVI. JEWEL CABINET.

Inlaid in rose and sycamore woods. Stamped "J. H. Riesener."
Chased Ormoulu mountings by Gouthière.

(*Jones Bequest. Victoria and Albert Museum.*)

14

The artificial pretence at Arcadian simplicity adopted by the Queen, in the intervals between her attendance at public *bals-masqué*, when she almost wantonly outraged the susceptibilities of the French people by her frivolities, found a more permanent form in interior decorations. Riesener and David designed a great deal of furniture for her. Dainty work-tables and writing-tables and other furniture of an elegant description are preserved in the national collection in the Louvre and at Fontainebleau, in the Victoria and Albert Museum in the Jones Bequest, and in the Wallace Collection. Tables of this nature are most eagerly sought after. A small table with plaques of porcelain in the side panels, which is said to have belonged to Marie Antoinette, was sold at Christie's for £6,000 (Hamilton Collection). There is a similar writing-table in the Jones Collection, given by Marie Antoinette to Mrs. Eden, afterwards Lady Auckland.

During the period under Louis Seize, when Fragonard and Natoire deftly painted the panels of rooms and filled ceilings with flying cupids and chains of roses, when Boucher was Director of the Academy, the interior of rooms assumed a boudoir-like appearance. The walls were decorated in a scheme of colour. Handsome fluted pillars with fine classic feeling were the framework of panelling painted in delicate and subdued tones. Oval mirrors, avoiding all massive construction, lightened the effect, and mantelpieces of white marble, and furniture evidently designed for use, completed the interiors of the homes of the *grands seigneurs.*   Sometimes the walls were painted, giving a lustrous appearance resembling silk, and this style is the forerunner of the modern abomination known as wall-paper.

Before leaving this period of French furniture, when so much marquetry work was done of unsurpassed beauty and of unrivalled technique, a word may be said as to the number of woods used. Oeben and Riesener and their contemporaries used many foreign woods, of which the names are unfamiliar. Mr. Pollen, in his " South Kensington Museum Handbook to Furniture and Woodwork," has given the names of some of them, which are interesting as showing the number of woods especially selected for this artistic cabinetmaking.   Tulip-wood is the variety known as *Liriodendron tulipifera.* Rosewood was extensively used, and holly (*ilex aquifolium*), maple (*acer campestre*), laburnum (*cytisus Alpinus*), and purple wood (*copaifera pubiflora*).   Snake-wood was frequently used, and other kinds of light-brown wood in which the natural grain is waved or curled, presenting a pleasant appearance, and obviating the use of marquetry (*see* " Woods used," p. 29).

In the great collections to which reference has been made, in well-known pieces made by Riesener his name is found stamped on the panel itself, or sometimes on the oak lining. The large bureau in the Wallace Collection (Gallery xvi., No. 66) is both signed and dated " 20th February, 1769." This piece, it is said, was ordered by Stanislas Leczinski, King of Poland, and was once one of the possessions of the Crown of France.

With regard to the cost of pieces of furniture by the great master *ébénistes*, it is on record that a secretaire which was exhibited at Gore House in 1853, and made originally for Beaumarchais by Riesener, cost 85,000 francs, a sum not much less than £4,000. Celebrated copies have been made from these old models. The famous cabinet

By permission of
Messrs. Waring.

LOUIS XVI. RIESENER COMMODE

with mounts by Gouthière, now in the possession of the King, was copied about twenty-five years ago for the Marquis of Hertford, by permission of Queen Victoria. The piece took years to complete, and it is interesting to have the evidence of its copyists that the most difficult parts to imitate were the metal mounts. This replica cost some £3,000, and is now in the Wallace Collection. The copy of the famous bureau or escritoire in the Louvre, known as the "Bureau de St. Cloud," was made by permission of the Emperor Napoleon III., and cost £2,000. Another copy of the same piece exhibited at the French International Exhibition was sold for £3,500 to an English peeress. Many fine copies of Riesener's work exist, and in the illustration (p. 197) a copy is given of a handsome commode, which exhibits his best style under the influence of his master, Oeben.

SALE PRICES.

£ s. d.

Suite of Louis XVI. furniture, with
fluted borders and legs, painted
white and pale green, the seats,
backs, and arms covered with old
Beauvais tapestry, with vases and
festoons of flowers and conven-
tional arabesques in polychrome,
on white ground in pale green borders, consisting of an oblong settee,
72 in. wide, eight fauteuils. Christie,
December 18, 1903 .   .   .   . 1470 0 0

Louis XVI. Parqueterie Encoignure,
with one door in the front, inlaid
with panels of rosettes and trelliswork on satin- and tulip-wood
ground, mounted with ormolu
corners, and surmounted by a
veined white marble slab, 25 in.
wide, stamped L. Wolff, ME.
Christie, July 8, 1920 .   .   .   63 0 0

Table, Louis XVI., marquetry, signed
" N. Petit," top inlaid with musical
trophy, &c., mounts, &c., of ormolu, cast and chased, 30 in. wide.
Christie, March 18, 1904 .   .   .   99 15 0

Commode, Louis XVI., stamped with
the name of " J. H. Reisener," with

tambour panels in front and drawers   £   s.   d.
at the top ; it is chiefly composed
of mahogany, the central panel inlaid in a coloured marquetry ; on
either side, and at the ends, are
panels of tulip-wood parquetery,
the whole is mounted with ormolu,
surmounted by a slab of veined
marble, 34 in. wide. Christie, May
27, 1904 3150   0   0

Louis XVI. Writing-Table, of mahogany, inlaid with panels of rosettes
and trelliswork in marqueterie, and
mounted with an ormolu frieze
chased with foliage and ribands,
the top covered with green leather,
58 in. wide, stamped P. Roussel
ME.   Property of Duke of Leeds.
Christie, June 10, 1920 . . . 1576   0   0

Louis XVI. Commode, with three
drawers in the frieze and two long
drawers below, inlaid with panels
of trelliswork in tulip-, satin-wood,
and ebony on mahogany ground,
and mounted with ormolu borders,
corners and frieze finely chased with
acanthus foliage, rosettes and beading surmounted by a veined grey
marble slab, 58 in. wide, stamped
" J. H. Riesener."   From the Garde

	£	s.	d.
Meuble, Fontainebleau. Arnold Collection. Christie, June 8, 1920 .	4515	0	0

Louis XVI. Fauteuils (Four), the frame-works carved with foliage, beading and fluting, and painted white, the seats, backs and arms stuffed, and covered with Beauvais tapestry woven with baskets and wreaths of flowers entwined with blue ribands on cream ground. Harland-Peck Sale. Christie, June 23, 1920 . . 1785   0   0

Louis XVI. Marqueterie Commode, with three doors in the front en-closing drawers, inlaid with vases of flowers, figures and buildings in marqueterie of various woods, with tulip- and hare-wood borders, mounted with ormolu corners, bor-ders and leg-mounts chased with laurel-festoons, foliage and beading, and surmounted by a veined grey marble slab, 52 in. wide, stamped " F. Raver, ME." Christie, July 8, 1920 462   0   0

IX

FRENCH FURNITURE. THE FIRST EMPIRE STYLE

CONTEMPORARY WITH THE CONCLUDING
YEARS OF THE REIGN OF GEORGE III.

EMPIRE CHAIR.

PORTRAIT OF MADAME RÉCAMIER.
(After David.)

Showing Empire settee and footstool.

(*In the Louvre.*)

IX

FRENCH FURNITURE—THE FIRST EMPIRE STYLE

1789. Commencement of French Revolution.

1798. Napoleon's campaign in Egypt.

1805. Napoleon prepares to invade England ; Battle of Trafalgar ; French naval power destroyed.

1806. Napoleon issued Berlin Decree to destroy trade of England.

1812. Napoleon invaded Russia, with disastrous retreat from Moscow.

1814. Napoleon abdicated.

1815. Wellington defeated Napoleon at Waterloo.

WHEN Louis XVI. called together the States-General in 1789, which had not met since 1614, the first stone was laid of the French Republic.

After the king was beheaded in 1793, the Reign of Terror followed, during which the wildest licence prevailed. Under the Directory, for four years from 1795, the country settled down until the rise of Napoleon Bonaparte, who took the government in his own hands with the title of Consul, and in 1804 called himself Emperor of the French.

During the Reign of Terror the ruthless fury of a nation under mob-law did not spare the most beautiful objects of art which were associated with a hated aristocracy. Furniture especially suffered, and it is a matter for wonderment that so much escaped destruction. Most of the furniture of the royal palaces was consigned to the spoliation of " the Black Committee," who trafficked in works of great price, and sold to foreign dealers the gems of French art for less than a quarter of their real value. So wanton had become the destruction of magnificent furniture that the Convention, with an eye on the possibilities of raising money in the future, ordered the furniture to be safely stored in the museums of Paris.

After so great a social upheaval, art in her turn was subjected to revolutionary notions. Men cast about to find something new. Art, more than ever, attempted to absorb the old classic spirit. The Revolution was the deathblow to Rococo ornament. With the classic influences came ideas from Egypt, and the excavations at Herculaneum and Pompeii provided a further source of design. A detail of a portion of a tripod table found at Pompeii shows the nature of the beautiful furniture discovered.

As early as 1763, Grimm wrote: "For some years past we are beginning to inquire for antique ornaments and forms. The interior and exterior decorations of houses, furniture, materials of dress, work of the goldsmiths, all bear alike the stamp of the Greeks. The fashion passes from architecture to millinery; our ladies have their hair dressed *à la Grecque*." A French translation of Winckelmann appeared in 1765, and Diderot lent his powerful aid in heralding the dawn of the revival of the antique long before the curtain went up on the events of 1789.

Paris in Revolution days assumed the atmosphere of ancient Rome. Children were given Greek and Roman names. Classical things got rather mixed. People called themselves "Romans." Others had Athenian notions. Madame Vigée-Lebrun gave *soupers à la Grecque*. Madame Lebrun was Aspasia, and M. l'Abbé Barthélemy, in a Greek dress with a laurel wreath on his head, recited a Greek poem.

DETAIL OF TRIPOD TABLE FOUND AT POMPEII.

(*At Naples Museum.*)

These, among a thousand other signs of the extraordinary spirit of classicism which possessed France, show how deep rooted had become the idea of a modern Republic that should emulate the fame of Athens and of Rome. The First

Consul favoured these ideas, and his portraits represent him with a laurel wreath around his head posing as a Cæsar.

In transition days before the style known as Empire had become fixed there is exhibited in art

By kind permission from the collection of Dr. Sigerson, Dublin.

SERVANTE.

Marble top ; supported on two ormoulu legs elaborately chased with figures of Isis. Panelled at back with glass mirror.

FRENCH ; LATE EIGHTEENTH CENTURY.

a feeling which suggests the deliberate search after new forms and new ideas. To this period belongs the *servante*, which, by the kindness of Dr. Sigerson, of Dublin, is reproduced from his collection.

The claw-foot, the ram's head, the bay-leaf, and a

JEWEL CABINET OF THE EMPRESS MARIE LOUISE.

Made on the occasion of her marriage with the Emperor Napoleon Bonaparte, in 1810.

(*At Fontainebleau.*)

frequent use of caryatides and animal forms, is a common ornamentation in furniture of the Empire

15

period. In this specimen the two legs of ormolu have these characteristics, and it is noticeable that the shape of the leg and its details of ornament bear a striking resemblance to the leg of the Pompeiian table illustrated (p. 205). But the deities of Egypt have contributed a new feature in the seated figure of the goddess Isis.

Napoleon himself encouraged the classic spirit which killed all memories of an *ancien régime*. He would have been pleased to see all the relics of the former glories of France demolished. He had at one time a project to rebuild Versailles as a classic temple.

At the height of his splendour he became the patron of the fine arts, and attempted to leave his impression upon art as he did upon everything else. New furniture was designed for the Imperial palaces. Riesener was alive, but it does not appear that he took any part in the new creations. David, the great French painter, an ardent Republican, was won over to become a Court painter. At Malmaison and at Fontainebleau there are many fine examples of the First Empire period which, however, cannot be regarded as the most artistic in French furniture. Preserved at Fontainebleau is the jewel cabinet, made by Thomire and Odiot, at the Emperor's orders as a wedding gift, in 1810, to the Empress Marie Louise, in emulation of the celebrated Riesener cabinet at the Trianon. The wood used for this, and for most of the Empire cabinets, is rich mahogany, which affords a splendid ground for the bronze gilt mounts (*see* p. 207).

The portrait of Madame Récamier, by David, which is in the Louvre, given as headpiece to this chapter, shows the severe style of furniture in use at the zenith of the Empire period. The couch follows classic models, and the tall candelabrum is a suggestion from Herculaneum models.

The influence that this classic revival had upon furniture in this country is told in a subsequent chapter. In regard to costume, the gowns of the First Empire period have become quite fashionable in recent years.

Although this style of furniture degenerated into commonplace designs with affectedly hard outlines, it had a considerable vogue. In addition to the influence it had upon the brothers Adam and upon Sheraton, it left its trace on English furniture up till the first quarter of the nineteenth century. The chair illustrated (p. 210) is about the year 1800 in date. There is presumptive evidence that this chair was made in Bombay after European design. It is of rosewood, carved in relief with honeysuckle and floral design. The scrolled ends of the top rail show at once its French derivation.

In the national collections in this country there are very few specimens of Empire furniture. The Duke of Wellington has some fine examples at Apsley House, treasured relics of its historic associations with the victor of Waterloo. The demand in France, for furniture of the First Empire style has in all probability denuded the open market of many fine specimens. Owing to the fact that this country was at war with France when the style was at its height, the number of Empire pieces imported was very limited, nor does First Empire furniture seem to have greatly captivated the taste of English collectors, as among the records of sales of furniture by public auction very little has come under the hammer.

ARMCHAIR, ROSEWOOD.

Carved in relief with honeysuckle pattern.
Formerly in possession of the Duke of Newcastle.

ENGLISH ; LATE EIGHTEENTH CENTURY.

X

CHIPPENDALE
AND
HIS STYLE

GEORGE II. (1727–1760)

GEORGE III. (1760–1820)

THOMAS CHIPPENDALE

Worked in London from about 1727 to 1779.

From 1772–1796 the firm was Chippendale & Haig.

Thomas Chippendale (son of the great Chippendale) continued
the business till 1820.

TABLE MADE BY CHIPPENDALE.

(Height, 29⅜ in.; width, 32⅜ in.; depth, 21⅝ in.)

X

CHIPPENDALE AND HIS STYLE

George I.	. . .	1714–1727.
George II.	. . .	1727–1760.
George III.	. . .	1760–1820.

Horace Walpole built Strawberry Hill (1750)

Sir William Chambers (1726–1796) built Pagoda at Kew about 1760.

Chippendale's *Director* published (1754).

THOMAS CHIPPENDALE, the master cabinetmaker of St. Martin's Lane, has left a name which, like that of

Boule, has become a trade term to mark a certain style in furniture. With the dawn of the age of mahogany, Chippendale produced designs that were especially adapted to the new wood ; he relied solely upon the delicate carving for ornament, and rejected all inlay.

Discovered by Sir Walter Raleigh, who brought specimens home with him, mahogany did not come into general use till about 1720. The material then used by Chippendale and his school was the splendid mahogany from the great untouched forests, producing at that time timber the like of which, in dimension and in quality, is now unprocurable. The cheaper "Honduras stuff" was then unknown, and English crews landed and cut timber from the Spanish possessions in spite of the protests of the owners. Many a stiff fight occurred, and many lives were lost in shipping this stolen mahogany to England to supply the demand for furniture. These nefarious proceedings more than once threatened to bring about war between England and Spain.

The furniture of France, during the four great periods treated in the previous chapters, was designed for the use of the nobility. One wonders what furniture was in common use by the peasantry in France. In England, too, much of the furniture left for the examination of posterity was made for the use of the wealthy classes. In Jacobean days, settles and chairs, especially the Yorkshire and Derbyshire types, were in more common use, and the homely pieces of Queen Anne suggest less luxurious surroundings, but it was left for Chippendale to impress his taste upon all classes.   In the

OLIVER GOLDSMITH'S CHAIR.

Wood, painted green, with circular seat, carved arms, and high back. Bequeathed by Oliver Goldsmith in 1774 to his friend, Dr. Hawes.

(*Bethnal Green Museum.*)

title-page of his great work, the *Director*, published

in 1754, he says that his designs are "calculated to improve and refine the present taste, and suited to the fancy and circumstances of persons in all degrees of life."

His book of designs, as may naturally be supposed, was not greatly bought by the working classes, but fifteen copies of the *Director* went to Yorkshire, and many other copies were subscribed for in other parts of the country, so that local cabinetmakers began at once to fashion their furniture after his styles.

The common form of chair at the time was similar to the specimen illustrated (p. 215), which formerly belonged to Oliver Goldsmith, and was bequeathed by him to his friend, Dr. Hawes. This is of soft wood, probably beech, painted green, with circular seat, curved arms, and high back. Chippendale revolutionised this inartistic style, and for the first time in the history of the manufacture of furniture in England, continental makers turned their eyes to this country in admiration of the style in vogue here, and in search of new designs.

It might appear, on a hasty glance at some of Chippendale's work, that originality was not his strong point. His claw-and-ball feet were not his own, and he borrowed them and the wide, spacious seats of his chairs from the Dutch, or from earlier English furniture under Dutch influence.

Sir William Chambers, the architect of Somerset House, whose fondness for Chinese ornament produced quite a craze, and who built the Pagoda in Kew Gardens, gave Chippendale another source of inspiration. In his later days he came under the

CHIPPENDALE SETTEE; WALNUT. ABOUT 1740.

(From the collection of Sir W. E. Welby-Gregory, Bart.)

CHIPENDALE SETTEE, OAK. ABOUT 1740.

(*By courtesy of V. J. Robinson, Esq., C.I.E.*)

influence of the Gothic revival and was tempted to misuse Gothic ornament.

His second style shows the Louis XIV. French decoration in subjection. In his ribbon-back chairs he employed the Louis XVI. ornamentation.

But Chippendale was the most masterly adapter that England has ever produced. His adaptions became original under his hand, and his creations are sturdy and robust, tempered by French subtleties, and having, here and there, as in the fretwork in the chair-legs and angles, a suggestion of the East. He is the prince of chair-makers. His chairs are never unsymmetrical. He knew the exact proportion of ornament that the structure would gracefully bear. The splats in the chairs he made himself are of such accurate dimensions in relation to the open spaces on each side that this touch alone betrays the hand of the master, which is absent in the imitations of his followers.

The illustration given of the Chippendale table in Chinese style (p. 213), is a beautiful and perfect piece of a type rarely met with. It was made by Chippendale for the great-grandmother of the present owner A similar table was in the possession of the Princess Josephine. In chairs, the back was sometimes of fret-cut work, as was also the design of the legs, with fretwork in the angles, which betray his fondness for the Chinese models. The Gothic style influenced Chippendale only to a slight degree. Horace Walpole at Strawberry Hill set the fashion in England, which fortunately was short-lived.

Collectors divide Chippendale's work into three

periods. To the first they assign the more solid chairs or settees with cabriole legs and Louis XIV. ornament, harmoniously blended with Queen Anne style. These chairs and settees are often found with claw-and-ball feet, and are frequently of walnut. Two fine examples of settees, the one of oak, the other of walnut, are illustrated.

RIBBON PATTERN. CHIPPENDALE CHAIR-BACK.

(From the " Director.")

The second period embraces the fine creations which have the celebrated Louis XVI. ribbon ornamentation in the backs. From one of the designs in Chippendale's book, here illustrated, the elegance of the style is shown. It is exuberant enough, but the author complains in his volume that " In executing many of these drawings, my pencil has but faintly carved out those images my fancy suggested ; but in this failure I console myself by reflecting that the greatest masters of every art have laboured under the same difficulties." The ribbon-backed chair illustrated (p. 223) is one of the two given to an ancestor of the present owner by the fourth Duke of Marlborough in 1790. They were formerly at Blenheim, and there is an added interest in them owing to the fact that the seats were worked by Sarah, the great Duchess of Marlborough.

RIBBON-BACKED CHIPPENDALE CHAIR, FORMERLY AT BLENHEIM,
THE SEAT WORKED BY SARAH, DUCHESS OF MARLBOROUGH.

The latest style of Chippendale's work is the Gothic. There are many pieces in existence which he probably had to produce to satisfy the taste of his fashionable clients, but the style is atrocious, and

CHIPPENDALE CORNER CHAIR, ABOUT 1780.

(From the collection of the late Hon. Sir Spencer Ponsonby-Fane, G.C.B., I.S.O.)

the less said about them the better. The illustration (p. 226) of a chair-back from his design-book shows how offensive it could be.

The fine corner-chair, here illustrated, exhibits the

DESIGN FOR MAHOGANY TABLE BY HEPPLEWHITE.

Reproduced from A. Hepplewhite & Co.'s "Cabinet Maker and Upholsterer's Guide," 1794 (3rd edition).

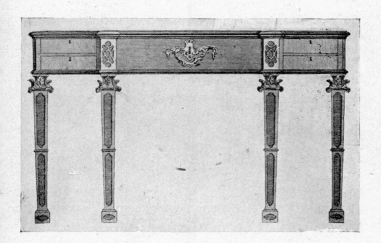

DESIGN FOR MAHOGANY TABLE BY CHIPPENDALE.

Reproduced from Thomas Chippendale's "The Gentleman and Cabinet Maker's Director," 1754.

strength and solidity he could impart to his work. His chairs were meant to sit upon, and are of excellent carpentry. The square, straight legs are a feature of much of his work. The examples belonging to the India Office and the Governors of the Charterhouse illustrated (p. 227) show the type that he made his own and with which his name has been associated.

Although his chairs are sought after as especially beautiful in design (his father was a maker of chairs before him) he made many other objects of furniture. The mirrors he designed are exquisite examples of fine woodcarving. The one illustrated (p. 229) shows the mastery he had over graceful outline.

GOTHIC CHIPPENDALE CHAIR-BACK.

(*From the " Director."*)

Bureau bookcases with drop-down fronts have been successfully produced since his day after his models. The one illustrated (p. 231) shows a secret drawer, which is reached by removing the left-hand panel. Card-tables, settees, knife-boxes, tea-caddies, sideboards, and overmantles were made by him, which show by their diversity of technique that there was more than one pair of hands at work in carrying out his designs.

The collecting of Chippendale furniture has become

By courtesy of proprietors of the "Connoisseur."

MAHOGANY CHIPPENDALE CHAIR. ABOUT 1740.

(The Property of the India Office.)

MAHOGANY CHIPPENDALE CHAIR. 1770.

(The property of the Charterhouse.)

so fashionable that two chairs at Christie's realised eleven hundred pounds some years ago.

Chippendale, the shopkeeper, of St. Martin's Lane, who took orders for furniture, which he or his sons, or workmen under their direct supervision executed, was one person, and Chippendale, who had quarrelled with the Society of Upholsterers, and published a book of designs on his own account, which quickly ran through three editions, was another person. In the one case he was a furniture maker whose pieces bring enormous prices. In the other he was the pioneer of popular taste and high-priest to the cabinetmakers scattered up and down England, who quickly realised the possibilities of his style, and rapidly produced good work on his lines.

These pieces are by unknown men, and no doubt much of their work has been accredited to Chippendale himself. The illustration (p. 232) shows a mahogany chair well constructed, of a time contemporary with Chippendale and made by some smaller maker. This type of chair has been copied over and over again till it has become a recognised pattern. It finds its counterpart in china in the old willow-pattern, which originated at Coalport and has been adopted as a stock design.

Furniture is not like silver, where the mark of the maker was almost as obligatory as the hall mark. Artists, both great and small, have signed their pictures, and in the glorious days of the great French *ébénistes* and metal-chasers, signed work is frequently found. But in England, at a time when furniture of excellent design, of original conception, and of

CHIPPENDALE MIRROR.

thoroughly good workmanship was produced in great quantities, the only surviving names are those of designers or cabinetmakers who have published books.

So great was the influence of the style of Chip-

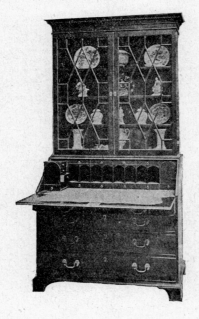

CHIPPENDALE BUREAU BOOKCASE.
With drop-down front, showing secret drawer.

pendale that it permeated all classes of society.   An interesting engraving by Stothard (p. 235) shows the interior of a room, and is dated 1782, the year that Rodney gained a splendid victory over the French fleet in the West Indies, and the year that saw the independence of the United States recognised.

Kitchen furniture or cottage furniture was made on the same lines by makers all over the country.   The wood used was not mahogany; it was most frequently

MAHOGANY CHAIR.

IN THE CHIPPENDALE STYLE.   LATE
EIGHTEENTH CENTURY.

beech. Chairs of this make are not museum examples, but they are not devoid of a strong artistic feeling, and are especially English in character.   More often than not the soft wood of this class of chair is found

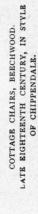

COTTAGE CHAIRS, BEECHWOOD.
LATE EIGHTEENTH CENTURY, IN STYLE
OF CHIPPENDALE.

to be badly worm-eaten. Two chairs of this type, of beech, are illustrated (p. 233), and it is interesting to note that, as in the instance of the Yorkshire and Derbyshire chairs of Jacobean days made by local makers, it is not common to find many of exactly

INTERIOR OF ROOM, ABOUT 1782.

(*From engraving after Stothard.*)

the same design. The craftsman gave a personal character to his handiwork, which makes such pieces of original and artistic interest, and cabinet-making and joinery was not then so machine-made as it is now.

It may be here remarked that the earlier pieces of the eighteenth century were polished much in the same manner as was old oak previously described. Highly polished surfaces and veneers, and that abomination " French polish," which is a cheap and nasty method of disguising poor wood, bring furniture within the early nineteenth-century days, when a wave of Philistine banalties swept over Europe.

SALE PRICES.

<table>
<tr><td></td><td>£</td><td>s.</td><td>d.</td></tr>
<tr><td>Circular Table, with escalloped top, the border carved with shells and gadrooning on open tripod carved with eagles' heads, and with ball-and-claw feet. 32 ins. diameter. Dean Sale. Christie, June 14, 1909 . . . .</td><td>315</td><td>0</td><td>0</td></tr>
<tr><td>Settee, Chippendale, mahogany, with triple back pierced and carved with oak branches entwined with ribands and framed by C-shaped scrolls; the arms carved with branches and terminate in grotesque birds' heads; the border of the seat carved in the centre with a mask and with shells and branches on each side; on cabriole legs with claw feet. Dean Sale. Christie, June 14, 1909 . .</td><td>2047</td><td>10</td><td>0</td></tr>
<tr><td>Chairs, set of six mahogany, the backs of Queen Anne design, slightly carved with foliage, the seat bordered by a frieze of key pattern; legs carved as lions' legs with ball-and-claw feet. Dean Sale. Christie, June 14, 1909 . . . . .</td><td>367</td><td>10</td><td>0</td></tr>
</table>

Settee, Chippendale mahogany, with double back with scroll top, carved

£   s.   d.

with arabesque foliage, the arms
terminating in masks, on legs
carved with lions' masks and claw
feet, 54 in. wide. Christie, April 12,
1904   278   5   0

Mirror, Chippendale, carved with gilt,
88 in. high, 50 in. wide. Christie,
May 18, 1904 . . . . .   94 10   0

Suite of Chippendale Mahogany Furniture, with straight legs and stretchers, the seats and backs stuffed,
and covered with needlework with
panels of figure subjects, animals
and flowers in coloured silks on
white and black ground, consisting
of a settee, 5 ft. 3 in. wide, and six
chairs. Christie, July 8, 1920 .   . 1234 16   0

Eleven Chippendale Mahogany Armchairs, the arm - supports and
straight legs carved with lattice-
work, the seats and backs stuffed,
and two of the seats and three of
the backs covered with the original
needlework, with figures and
flowers in coloured silks and wool.
Christie, July 8, 1920 . . . 1212 15   0

Chippendale Mahogany Side-table, with
fluted frieze, the cabriole legs carved
with foliage and claw feet, 49 in.
wide. Christie, July 8 1920 .   .   89   5   0

	£	s.	d.
Chippendale Mahogany Cabinet, with glazed folding doors in the upper part and cupboards below, with panelled doors enclosing shelves, the cornice carved with lattice-work, 7 ft. 5 in. high, 4 ft. 7 in. wide. Christie, July 8, 1920 . . .	126	0	0
Chinese Chippendale Armchairs, square backs of fret pattern on square legs connected with a similar pattern at front and sides, with loose seats. Messrs. Sotheby, June 21, 1920	62	0	0
Set of Six Irish Chippendale Mahogany Elbow Chairs, the ladder backs with pierced panels, and with shaped elbows, on fluted square legs and stretchers. Puttick & Simpson, February 27, 1920 . . .	75	12	0

17

XI

SHERATON, ADAM, AND HEPPLEWHITE STYLES

THOMAS SHERATON (1775–1793)

"Cabinet Maker and Upholsterer's Drawing Book," 1791–1794.

ROBERT ADAM
JAMES ADAM

Classic influence in architecture and furniture began about 1760.

A. HEPPLEWHITE & CO.

"Cabinet Maker and Upholsterer's Guide," 1788.

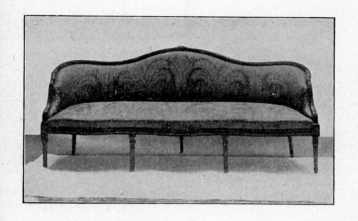

HEPPLEWHITE SETTEE, MAHOGANY.

XI

SHERATON, ADAM, AND HEPPLEWHITE STYLES

Robert Adam . . 1728–1792.
Thomas Sheraton . 1751–1806.

1752. Loch and Copeland's designs published.
1765. Manwaring's designs published.
1770. Ince and Mayhew's designs published.
1788. Hepplewhite's designs published.

IN the popular conception of the furniture of the three Georges the honours are divided between Chippendale and Sheraton. Up till recently all that was not Chippendale was Sheraton, and all that was not Sheraton must be Chippendale. The one is represented by the straight-legged mahogany chairs or cabriole legs with claw-and-ball feet and the backs elaborately carved ; the other with finely tapered legs, built on elegant lines, and of satinwood, having marquetry decoration or painted panels.

This is the rough generalisation that obtained in the earlier days of the craze for collecting eighteenth-century furniture. Hepplewhite and Adam (more often than not alluded to as Adams), are now added to the list, and auction catalogues attempt to differentiate accordingly. But these four names do not represent a quarter of the well-known makers who were producing good furniture in the days between the South Sea Bubble in 1720 and the battle of Waterloo in 1815.

In this chapter it will be impossible to give more than a passing allusion to the less-known makers of the eighteenth century, but to those who wish to pursue the matter in more detailed manner the Bibliography annexed (p. 19) gives ample material for a closer study of the period.

The four brothers Adam, sons of a well-known Scottish architect, were exponents of the classic style Robert Adam was the architect of the fine houses in the Adelphi, and he designed the screen and gateway at the entrance to the Admiralty in 1758. James is credited with the designing of interior decorations and furniture. Carriages, sedan-chairs, and even plate were amongst the artistic objects to which these brothers gave their stamp. The classical capitals, mouldings and niches, the shell

SHERATON ARMCHAIR;
MAHOGANY, ABOUT 1780.

ADAM ARMCHAIR;
MAHOGANY, ABOUT 1790.

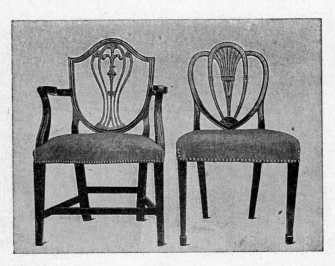

ARMCHAIR OF WALNUT, SHIELD-
BACK CARVED WITH THREE
OSTRICH FEATHERS. IN HEPPLE-
WHITE STYLE. LATE EIGH-
TEENTH CENTURY.

CHAIR OF WALNUT, SHIELD-
BACK; IN THE STYLE OF
HEPPLEWHITE. LATE
EIGHTEENTH CENTURY.

(Victoria and Albert Museum.)

flutings and the light garlands in the Adam style, are welcome sights in many otherwise dreary streets in London. Robert, the eldest brother, lived from 1728 to 1792, and during that time exercised a great influence on English art.

In 1790, a set of designs of English furniture were published by A. Hepplewhite. In these chairs with pierced backs, bookcases with fancifully framed glass doors, and mahogany bureaux, the influence of Chippendale is evident, but the robustness of the master and the individuality of his style become transformed into a lighter and more elegant fashion, to which French *finesse* and the Adam spirit have contributed their influence.

In the illustration (p. 243) various types of chairs of the period are given. A chair termed the "ladder-back" was in use in France at the same time. In Chardin's celebrated picture of " *Le jeu de l'oye*," showing the interior of a parlour of the middle eighteenth century, a chair of this type is shown.

The Hepplewhite settee illustrated as the headpiece to this chapter shows the delicate fluting in the woodwork, and the elaborated turned legs which were beginning to be fashionable at the close of the eighteenth century. The two chairs by Hepplewhite & Co., illustrated (p. 243), are typical examples of the elegance of the style which has an individuality of its own—a fact that collectors are beginning to recognise.

The shield-back chair with wheat-ear and open-work decoration, and legs in which the lathe has been freely used, are characteristic types. The elegance of the legs in Hepplewhite chairs is especially noticeable. The designers departed from Chippendale with results exquisitely symmetrical, and of most graceful ornamentation.

Hogarth, in his biting satires on the absurdities of Kent, the architect, painter, sculptor, and ornamental gardener, whose claims to be any one of the four rest on slender foundations, did not prevent fashionable ladies consulting him for designs for furniture, picture frames, chairs, tables, for cradles, for silver plate, and even for the construction of a barge. It is recorded by Walpole that two great ladies who implored him to design birthday gowns for them were decked out in incongruous devices : " the one he dressed in a petticoat decorated in columns of the five orders, and the other like a bronze, in a copper-coloured satin, with ornaments of gold."

Hepplewhite learned the lesson of Hogarth, that " the line of beauty is a curve," and straight lines were studiously avoided in his designs. Of the varieties of chairs that he made, many have the Prince of Wales's feathers either carved upon them in the centre of the open-work back or japanned upon the splat, a method of decoration largely employed in France, which has not always stood the test of time, for when examples are found they often want restoration. Of satin-wood, with paintings upon the panels, Hepplewhite produced some good examples, and when he attempted greater elaboration his style in pieces of involved design and intricacy of detail became less original, and came into contact with Sheraton. His painted furniture commands

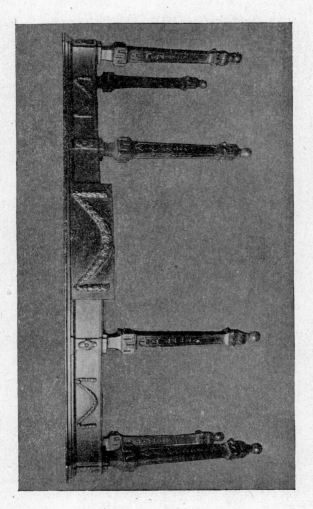

MAHOGANY CARVED SIDE TABLE. ROBERT ADAM PERIOD.

Exhibiting strong classic feeling and architectural *motifs* in carved decoration.

Height, 2 ft. 11 in.; length, 7 ft. 4½ in.; depth, 2 ft. 6½ in.

high prices, and the name of Hepplewhite will stand as high as Chippendale or Sheraton for graceful interpretations of the spirit which invested the late eighteenth century.

Before dealing with Sheraton in detail, the names of some lesser known makers contemporary with him may be mentioned. Matthias Lock, together with a cabinetmaker named Copeland, published in 1752 designs of furniture which derived their inspiration from the brothers Adam, which classic feeling later, in conjunction with the Egyptian and Pompeian spirit, dominated the style of the First Empire. Josiah Wedgwood, with his Etruscan vases, and Flaxman, his designer, filled with the new classic spirit, are examples in the world of pottery of the influences which were transmitted through the French Revolution to all forms of art when men cast about in every direction to find new ideas for design.

Ince and Mayhew, two other furniture designers, published a book in 1770, and Johnson outdid Chippendale's florid styles in a series of designs he brought out, which, with their twisted abortions, look almost like a parody of Thomas Chippendale's worst features. There is a "Chairmaker's Guide," by Manwaring and others in 1766, which contains designs mainly adapted from all that was being produced at the time. It is not easy to tell the difference between chairs made by Manwaring and those made by Chippendale, as he certainly stands next to the great master in producing types which have outlived ephemeral tastes, and taken their stand as fine artistic creations.

Among other names are those of Shearer, Darly, and Gillow, all of whom were notable designers and makers of furniture in the period immediately preceding the nineteenth century.

Thomas Sheraton, contemporary with William Blake the dreamer, shares with him the unfortunate posthumous honour of reaching sensational prices in auction rooms. There is much in common between the two men. Sheraton was born in 1751 at Stockton-on-Tees, and came to London to starve. Baptist preacher, cabinetmaker, author, teacher of drawing, he passed his life in poverty, and died in distressed circumstances. He was, before he brought out his book of designs, the author of several religious works. Often without capital to pursue his cabinetmaking he fell back on his aptitude for drawing, and gave lessons in design. He paid young Black, who afterwards became Lord Provost of Edinburgh, half a guinea a week as workman in his cabinetmaker's shop in Soho. In a pathetic picture of those days the Lord Provost, in his *Memoirs*, tells how Sheraton and his wife and child had only two cups and saucers and the child had a mug, and when the writer took tea with them the wife's cup and saucer were given up to the guest, and she drank her tea from a common mug. This reads like Blake's struggles when he had not money enough to procure copper-plates on which to engrave his wonderful visions.

That the styles of Chippendale and Sheraton represent two distinct schools is borne out by what Sheraton himself thought of his great predecessor. Speaking in his own book of Chippendale's previous work he says : " As for the designs themselves they are wholly antiquated, and laid aside, though possessed of great merit according to the times in which they were executed." From this it would appear that the Chippendale style, at the time of Sheraton's " Cabinet-maker's and Upholsterer's Drawing Book," published in 1793, had gone out of fashion.

The woods mostly employed by Sheraton were satinwood, tulip-wood, rosewood, and apple-wood, and occasionally mahogany. In place of carved scrollwork he used marquetry, and on the cabinets and larger pieces panels were painted by Cipriani and Angelica Kauffman. There is a fine example of the latter's work in the Victoria and Albert Museum.

Sheraton borrowed largely from the French style under Louis XVI., when the lines had become severer ; he came, too, under the influence of the Adam designs. He commonly used turned legs, and often turned backs, in his chairs. His later examples had a hollowed or spoon back to fit the body of the sitter. When he used mahogany he realised the beauty of effect the dark wood would give to inlay of lighter coloured woods, or even of brass. The splats and balusters, and even the legs of some of his chairs, are inlaid with delicate marquetry work.

Ornament for its own sake was scrupulously eschewed by Sheraton. The essential supports and uprights and stretcher-rails and other component parts of a piece of furniture were only decorated as portions of a preconceived whole. The legs were tapered, the plain surfaces were inlaid with marquetry,

but nothing meaningless was added.   In France
Sheraton's style was termed "*Louis Seize à l'Anglaise.*"

It was the firm of Hepplewhite that first intro-

OLD ENGLISH SECRÉTAIRE.

Rosewood and satinwood. Drop-down front.

duced the painted furniture into England, and under
Sheraton it developed into an emulation of the
fine work done by Watteau and Greuze in the days
of Marie Antoinette.

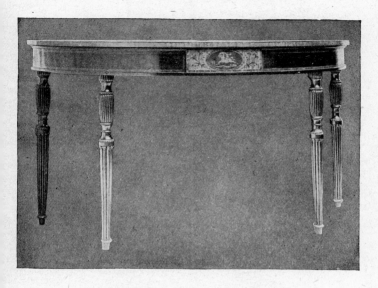

SHERATON SATINWOOD TABLE.

Showing strong indications of Adam influence.

With painted top and painted panel in front.

Detail of painted top of above table.

18

Among the varied pieces that Sheraton produced are a number of ingenious inventions in furniture, such as the library-steps he made for George III. to rise perpendicularly from the top of a table frame, and when folded up to be concealed within it.   His

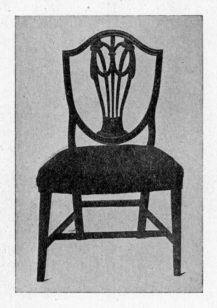

SHIELD-BACK CHAIR.   MAHOGANY.

LATE EIGHTEENTH CENTURY.

bureau-bookcases and writing-cabinets have sliding flaps and secret drawers and devices intended to make them serve a number of purposes.

On the front of his chairs is frequently found the

inverted bell flower, and another of his favourite forms of decoration is the acanthus ornament, which he puts to graceful use.

The influence of his work, and of that of Hepplewhite & Co., was lasting, and much of the late eighteenth century and early nineteenth century cabinetmaking owes its origin to their designs. The old English secrétaire illustrated (p. 250), of rose and satinwood, with drawer above and fall-down front, having cupboard beneath with doors finely inlaid with plaques of old lac, is of the date when Hepplewhite was successfully introducing this class of French work into England. It is especially interesting to note that the drawer-handles are mounted with old Battersea enamel.

The difficulty of definitely pronouncing as to the maker of many of the pieces of furniture of the late eighteenth century is recognised by experts. The chair illustrated (p. 251) cannot be assigned to any particular designer, though its genuine old feeling is indisputable. In the fine collection . of old furniture of this period at the Victoria and Albert Museum will be found many examples of chairs with no other title assigned to them than "late eighteenth century." This fact speaks for itself. A great and growing school had followed the precepts of Chippendale and Hepplewhite and Sheraton. This glorious period of little more than half a century might have been developed into a new Renaissance in furniture. Unfortunately, the early days of the nineteenth century and the dreary Early Victorian period, both before and after the great Exhibition of 1851, display the most tasteless ineptitude in nearly every branch of art. From the days of Elizabeth down to the last of the Georges, English craftsmen, under various influences, have produced domestic furniture of great beauty. It is impossible to feel any interest in the Windsor chair, the saddle-bag couch, or the red mahogany cheffonière. The specimens of misapplied work shown at the Bethnal Green Museum, relics of the English exhibits at the first Exhibition, are unworthy of great traditions.

The awakened interest shown by all classes in old furniture will do much to carry the designers back to the best periods in order to study the inheritance the masters have left, and it is to be hoped that the message of the old craftsmen dead and gone will not fall on deaf ears.

SALE PRICES.

	£	s.	d.
Chairs, wheel back, set of seven (including armchair), Adam, carved, mahogany. Good condition. Brady & Sons, Perth, September 1, 1902 .	27	2	6
Mirror, Adam, in gilt frame, Corinthian pillar sides, ornamental glass panel at top, surmounted by a carved wood eagle figure. Gudgeon & Sons, Winchester, November 11, 1903 .	7	10	0
Mirrors, pair, oval, Adam, carved and gilt wood frame. Christie, March 18, 1904	46	4	0
Side-tables, pair hare-wood, by Adam, with rounded corners, on square-shaped tapering legs, the sides and borders inlaid with marquetry, in coloured woods, 53 in. wide. Christie, June 2, 1904 . . .	105	0	0
Bookcase, 4 ft. 8 in., mahogany, Hepplewhite, inlaid tulip-wood with box and ebony lines, fitted shelves and drawers, enclosed by doors. Phillips, Son and Neale, November 17, 1903 , ...	44	0	0
Console-table, Hepplewhite, satinwood, the top shaped as a broken ellipse, and of hare-wood with inlays of			

husks and flowers round a fan-pattern centre with borderings in ebony and other woods on a filling of satinwood ; the edge is bound with ormolu, reeded and cross banded, below is the frieze of satinwood inlaid with honeysuckle, pateræ, and other ornament in holly, &c., and supported on a pair of carved square tapered legs painted and gilt, and with pendants of husks and acanthus capitals, 4 ft. 3 in. wide. Flashman & Co., Dover, April 26, 1904 . . .   40 0 0

Suite of Hepplewhite mahogany furniture, with open shield backs, with vase-shaped centres carved, the back, arms and legs widely fluted, consisting of a settee, 74 in. wide, and ten armchairs. Christie, June 2, 1904 . . . . . .   325 10 0

Knife-box, oblong, Sheraton mahogany, with revolving front, inlaid with Prince-of-Wales's feathers and borders in satinwood, 19½ in. wide. Christie, November 21, 1902 . .   7 17 6

Sideboard, Sheraton, mahogany, satinwood inlaid, fitted with brass rails. Dowell, Edinburgh, November 14, 1903 . . . .   30 9 0

	£	s.	d.
Wardrobe, Sheraton mahogany, banded with satinwood, with folding doors above and below, and five drawers in the centre, 7 ft. high, 8 ft. wide. Christie, January 22, 1904 . .	60	18	0
Armchairs, pair, Sheraton, with shield-shaped backs, painted with Prince of Wales's feathers, and pearl ornament on black ground. Christie, March 28, 1904	28	7	0
Cabinet, Sheraton satinwood, with glazed folding doors enclosing shelves, drawer in the centre forming secretary, and folding-doors below, painted with baskets of flowers, &c., 7 ft. 9 in. high, 41 in. wide. Christie, March 28, 1904 .	189	0	0
Sheraton Armchairs, pair with square backs carved ; on taper legs. Caned seats. With loose cushions in brocade. Messrs. Sotheby, June 21, 1920	52	0	0
Adam Mahogany Bookcase, with glazed doors in the upper part with vase-shaped panels and numerous drawers below, the cornice decorated with notched mouldings and surmounted by small vases, 9 ft. wide. Formerly the property of Warren Hastings. Christie, July 22, 1920 .	661	10	0

	£	s.	d.
Sheraton Satinwood Cabinet, with glazed folding doors in the upper part, drawer in the upper part forming secrétaire, drawers below and drawers and cupboards at the sides, banded with rosewood, and with mahogany cornice carved with fluting and rosettes, 4 ft. 9 in. wide. Christie, July 8, 1920 . . .	409	10	0
Hepplewhite Mahogany Armchair, with rounded back, the rails carved with palm-leaves, on tapering legs carved with rosettes and foliage. Christie, July 8, 1920 . . .	89	5	0
Six Hepplewhite Mahogany Chairs, with shield-shaped backs carved with Prince of Wales's plumes and drapery festoons, on tapering legs. Christie, July 8, 1920 . . .	120	15	0

XII

HINTS
TO COLLECTORS

DESIGN FOR SPURIOUS MARQUETRY WORK.

XII

HINTS TO COLLECTORS

THE demand for old furniture has become so great
that there is an increasing difficulty in supplying it.
In order to satisfy the collector many artifices have
been practised which in varying degree are difficult
to detect, according to the skill and ingenuity of the
present-day manufacturer of " antique " furniture.

Replicas of old pieces are frequently made, and
the workmanship is so excellent, and the copy of
the old craftsman's style so perfect, that it only
requires a century or two of wear to give to the
specimen the necessary tone which genuine old
furniture has naturally acquired.

In particular, French ornate furniture from the days of Boule to the Empire period has received the flattering attention of the fabricator by being imitated in all its details. These high-class French pieces are fine examples of cabinetmaking, and it is not easy for anybody who has not a special expert knowledge to pronounce definitely upon their authenticity. Doubts have even been expressed regarding certain pieces in the great national collections ; in fact the art of the forger in regard to old French furniture, of which specimens change hands at anything from £1,000 to £10,000, has reached a very high level of excellence, having almost been elevated to one of the fine arts. If a clever workman possessed of great artistic feeling turns his attention to forging works of art, it is obvious that his triumph is complete over amateurs possessed of less artistic taste and knowledge than himself.

Many secret processes are employed to impart an appearance of age to the wood and to the metal mountings. The cruder methods are to eat off the sharper edges of the metal mountings by means of acid, and to discolour the newer surfaces by the aid of tobacco juice, both of which are not difficult to detect. The steady manufacture of these finer pieces goes on in France, and it has been found that the foggy atmosphere of London is especially useful in producing the effect of age upon the finer work, consequently many forged pieces are shipped to London to be stored in order to ripen until considered fit for the American market, where so many forgeries have been planted. The reward is great,

"MADE-UP" BUFFET.

The middle portion, consisting of the two drawers and three panelled cupboards above, is genuine old carved oak. The stand, with the finely turned legs and rails, and the whole of the upper portion, is modern.

and even considering the amount of trouble bestowed upon such pieces and the excellence of the artistic work where the highest skilled labour is employed, the profit is enormous. The parvenu buys his Louis XIV. or Louis XV. suite, and pays an immense sum for pieces which are stated to have come from some French nobleman's château, whose name must not be divulged, and so the interesting deal is brought to a successful termination.

As an object-lesson as to the truth of the above remarks, the Wallace Collection contains a modern French copy in facsimile, by Dawson, of the celebrated " Bureau du Roi " of the Louis XV. period, the original being in the Louvre. The original is fully described in the chapter on Louis XV. style, and it is not too much to assert that ninety-nine per cent. of the visitors to the Collection could not say that this copy was not an old French specimen of over a century and a quarter ago, and the remaining one, unless he happened to be an expert, would not question its genuineness.

Old oak has always been a favourite with the public, and from the modern Flemish monstrosities, carved in evil manner and displaying proportions in the worst possible taste, to the equally vulgar home production in buffet or sideboard, and stocked by many dealers in so-called " antique " furniture, the number of grotesque styles foisted upon the public within the last fifteen years has been remarkable. One wonders what has become of the high-backed oak chairs, nearly black with repeated applications of permanganate of potash, having flaming red-leather seats. They seem to have mysteriously disappeared from up-to-date "antique" stores of late. The public has taken to inquiring into art matters a little more closely. Nowadays the latest thing is "fumed" oak, which is modern oak discoloured by means of ammonia, which darkens the surface of the wood to a depth of a sixteenth of an inch. It is not infrequent to find an attempt made to represent this as old oak after an elaborate treatment with linseed oil, turpentine, and beeswax, though an examination of the interior edges of the wood will discover its modernity at once.

Of course, such tricks as these are not practised by any firm of standing, who cannot afford to damage their reputation by any misrepresentation. As a general rule a dealer will readily point out the details of workmanship and offer technical information of much value to a beginner, if he discovers that his customer is a collector desirous of acquiring only fine specimens. It is more often than not the folly of the public, and not the dishonesty of the dealer, which results in trade frauds being committed in the attempt to execute some impossible and imperative order, which the moneyed collector has given. The difference between the genuine and the replica is most clearly made by old-fashioned firms of high standing. It is only when the collector enters into the arena and endeavours to set forth in quest of bargains, where he pits his skill against that of the dealer in the hope of outwitting the latter, that he is obviously on dangerous ground. In the one case he pays a higher price and obtains the benefit of the experience of a firm with expert knowledge, in the other he relies on his own judgment in picking up a bargain from some one whom he believes to be possessed of less knowledge than himself. If he is successful he is not slow to brag about his cleverness ; but if he is worsted in the encounter, and pays, let us say, five pounds for an object which he fondly believed was worth fifty, if genuine, and which he subsequently discovers is worth less than he gave, there is nothing too bad to say concerning his antagonist.

It is chiefly by the character of carved work that old pieces can be recognised. There are three classes of pitfalls to avoid.

1. Fraudulent pieces throughout, of modern wood and of modern carving.

2. " Made-up " pieces which often consist of genuine old pieces of carved wood pieced together ingeniously from fragments of carvings, with modern additions.

3. " Restored " pieces which are mainly old and should have received, if admitted to a collection, only the necessary repairs to make them serviceable.

With regard to the first class, fraudulent throughout, it is the hope of the writer that enough has already been written in this volume to point the way to the reader and to assist him to follow his natural inclinations in developing the necessary critical taste to readily detect pieces wholly false in character and feeling.

" Made-up " pieces present a greater difficulty. Considerable skill has been exercised in combining certain parts of old furniture into a whole which is, however, mostly inharmonious. In pieces of this nature there is an absence of feeling in style and carving. It is difficult to define the exact meaning of the word "feeling" as applied to art objects, it is a subtle expression of skill and poetry which communicates itself to the lover of art. It is so subtle and elusive that experts will tell one that such and such a piece requires to be "lived with" to test its authenticity. Mr. Frederick Roe, whose volume on "Ancient Coffers and Cupboards" displays a profound knowledge of his subject, writes, "it occasionally happens that pieces are so artfully made up that only living with them will enable the collector to detect the truth. In dealing with pieces of this suspicious kind one often has to fall back on a sort of instinct. With critical collectors of every sort this innate sense plays a very important part."

Two specimens of "made-up" furniture are reproduced, which will bear close study in order to appreciate the difficulty of collecting old oak.

The illustration of the buffet (p. 261) has many points of interest. The general appearance of the piece is not inharmonious. It has been carefully thought out and no less carefully put into effect. The middle portion, consisting of the three drawers and the three cupboards above, up to and including the shelf partition at the top, is the only old part. The handles, locks, and escutcheons of the two drawers are old, but the hinges above are modern copies of old designs, and the handles of the cupboards are modern replicas.

The massive stand with artistically turned rails in

MADE UP FROM
SEVERAL PIECES
OF GENUINE
OLD CARVED OAK.

CABINET OF
OLD OAK.

Jacobean style, is soft wood artfully fumed and generously beeswaxed. The whole of the top portion has been added and is soft wood very well carved. The carving of the panels is also well executed, and is evidently a copy of some old design.

The older portion is a fine piece of early Jacobean work, and it is not difficult to distinguish between the feeling of this and the expression conveyed by the modern woodwork. The patina of the wood after two centuries of exposure and polishing has that peculiarly pleasing appearance which accompanies genuine old woodwork. The edges of the carving have lost their sharp angles, and the mellowness of the middle panels are in strong contrast to the harsher tone of those of the upper portion.

Such a piece as this would not deceive an expert, nor, perhaps, is it intended to, or greater care would have been bestowed upon it, but it is sufficiently harmonious in composition not to offend in a glaring manner, and might easily deceive a tyro.

The next piece illustrated (p. 267) is interesting from another point of view. It is a more elaborate attempt to produce a piece of old furniture in which the details themselves have all the mellowness of fine old oak. In fact, with the exception of one portion, some eight inches by three, to which allusion will be made later, the whole of it is genuine old oak.

The three panels at the top are finely carved and are Jacobean work. The two outside panels at the bottom, though of a later period, are good work. The middle panel at the bottom is evidently a portion of a larger piece of carving, because the pattern abruptly breaks off, and it was most certainly not designed by the old carver to lie on its side in this fashion.

The two heads at the top corners have been cut from some old specimen, and artfully laid on. The carving on both sides, running below each head from top to bottom, is of two distinct designs joined in each case in a line level with the upper line of the lower panels. The two uprights on each side of the middle lower panel are exquisite pieces of carved work, but certainly never intended to be upright. They are evidently portions of a long, flowing ornament, as their cut-off appearance too plainly shows.

The top panels have done duty elsewhere, as part of the ornamental carving at the top and bottom of each lozenge is lost. The long line of scrolled carving above them is distinctly of interest. On the left hand, from the head to the middle of the panel, a piece of newer carving has been inserted, some eight inches long. The wood, at one time darkened to correspond with the adjacent carving, has become lighter, which is always the case when wood is stained to match other portions. The carving in this new portion follows in every detail the lines of the older design, and is a very pretty piece of "faking."

The cross-piece running from left to right, dividing the lower panels from the upper, is in three parts. An examination of the design shows that the last three circles on the right, and the last four on the left, are of smaller size than the others. The design evidently belonged to some other piece of furniture, and has been removed to do service in this "made-up" production.

In all probability the two uprights enclosing the top middle panel, and the two uprights on the outside at the bottom were once portions of a carved bedstead, as they are all of the same size and design. It is a notorious trick to slice an old carved bedpost into four pieces, skilfully fitting the pieces into "made-up" furniture.

There is a prevalent idea that worm-holes are actually produced in furniture, in order to give a new piece a more realistic appearance. There are traditions of duck-shot having been used, and there is little doubt that holes were drilled by makers who knew their public. But it is improbable that such artifices would be of much use for deceptive purposes nowadays. As a matter of fact, worm-holes are avoided by any one who gives a moment's thought to the matter. To get rid of worm in furniture is no easy task, and they eventually ruin any pieces they tenant.

The illustration (p. 274) shows a piece of Spanish chestnut badly honeycombed by furniture worms. In chairs, especially, their havoc is almost irreparable, and in the softer woods the legs become too rotten to be repaired or even strengthened. Metal plates are often screwed on the sides to prevent the chairs falling to pieces, but they become useless to sit upon without fear of disaster.

The insect is really the boring wood-beetle, which is armed with formidable forceps, to enable it to burrow through the wood. The worm, the larva of

19*

this beetle, is also provided with boring apparatus, and this insect, whether as beetle or as worm, is a deadly enemy to all furniture. The " death-watch " is also accused of being a depredator of books and of furniture of soft wood.

To remove worms from furniture is a costly undertaking, requiring the greatest skill. Large pieces of furniture have actually to be taken to pieces and the whole of the damaged parts removed with a chisel. In cases where the legs, or slender supports, have been attacked, the difficulty is one requiring the specialist's most delicate attention. Various applications are recommended, but cannot be stated to be reliable. Injecting paraffin is said to be the best remedy, and putting the pieces in a chamber where all the openings have been sealed, and lighting pans of sulphur underneath the furniture, allowing the specimens to remain in this fumigating bath for some days is another method resorted to.

With regard to Chippendale furniture, a word of caution is necessary. It is as impossible for Chippendale and his workmen to have produced all the furniture attributed to them as it is for the small factory at Lowestoft to have made all the china with which it is credited. As has been shown in the chapter on Thomas Chippendale, his styles were most extensively copied by his contemporaries all over the country and by many makers after him, and modern makers produce a great quantity of " Chippendale " every year. Only a careful examination of museum pieces will train the eye of the collector. The fine sense of proportion, at once noticeable in the genuine Chippendale chair, is absent in the modern copy, and, above all, the carving in the latter is thin and poor. In the old days the wastage of wood was not a thing which the master had in his mind. In modern copies the curl of the arm, or the swell at the top of the back, shows a regard for economy. There is a thin, flat look about the result, which ought not to be mistaken. Scrolls and ribbon-work are often added to later pieces made in the style of Chippendale, which have enough wood in their surfaces to bear carving away

DESIGN FOR
SPURIOUS MAR-
QUETRY WORK.

An ingenious device is adopted in cases of inlaid pieces of a small nature, such as imitation Sheraton clock-cases and knife-boxes and the frames of mirrors. Old engravings are procured of scroll-work, usually from the end of some book. The illustration (p. 259) shows the class of engravings selected. These engravings are coated with a very thin layer of vellum, which is boiled down to a liquid, and carefully spread over them. After this treatment they are ready to be glued on to the panels to be "faked," and, when coated over with transparent varnish, they present the appearance of an ivory and ebony inlay.

The frauds practised in satinwood and painted pieces are many and are exceedingly difficult to detect. Much of Sheraton's furniture was veneered with finely selected specimens of West India satinwood. These carefully chosen panels were painted by Cipriani and others. The modern "faker" has not the material to select from, as the satinwood imported is not so beautiful nor so richly varied in grain as in the old days. He removes a side panel from an old piece, and substitutes another where its obnoxious presence is not so noticeable. To this old panel he affixes a modern coloured print after one of Sheraton's artists, which, when carefully varnished over and skilfully treated so as to represent the cracks in the supposed old painting, is ready for insertion in the "made-up" sideboard, to catch the fancy of the unwary collector.

FINIS.

PIECE OF SPANISH CHESTNUT SHOWING
RAVAGES OF WORMS.

INDEX